'A Commonsense View of all Music'

'A COMMONSENSE VIEW OF ALL MUSIC'

Reflections on Percy Grainger's contribution to ethnomusicology and music education

JOHN BLACKING

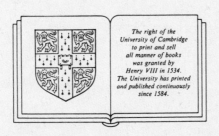

The right of the
University of Cambridge
to print and sell
all manner of books
was granted by
Henry VIII in 1534.
The University has printed
and published continuously
since 1584.

CAMBRIDGE UNIVERSITY PRESS

Cambridge
New York   Port Chester   Melbourne   Sydney

Published by the Press Syndicate of the University of Cambridge
The Pitt Building, Trumpington Street, Cambridge CB2 1RP
40 West 20th Street, New York, NY 10011, USA
10 Stamford Road, Oakleigh, Melbourne 3166, Australia

First published 1987
Reprinted 1989
First paperback edition 1990

Printed in Great Britain by
Redwood Burn Limited, Trowbridge, Wiltshire

British Library cataloguing in publication data

Blacking, John
'A commonsense view of all music':
reflections on Percy Grainger's contribution
to ethnomusicology and music education.
1.   Grainger, Percy Aldridge
I.   Title
780'.92'4   ML410.G75

Libary of Congress cataloguing in publication data

Blacking, John
'A commonsense view of all music'.
Bibliography.
1.   Grainger, Percy, 1882–1961 – Contributions in
ethnomusicology.   I.   Title.
ML410.G7B64   1987   781.7   87-6628

ISBN 0 521 26500 2 hard covers
ISBN 0 521 31924 2 paperback

For Robert Kauffman

Contents

Preface

I am greatly indebted to Sir Frank Callaway for the pleasure and the challenge of preparing this volume for publication. First, as Professor and Head of the Department of Music, he invited me to spend March to May of 1983 on the beautiful campus of the University of Western Australia, as Misha Strassberg Visiting Fellow. And secondly, he generously gave me a superb idea for my public lectures on ethnomusicological topics: he suggested that I should comment on what Percy Grainger had had to say about so-called 'folk' and 'non-Western' musics, and in particular on the synopsis of Grainger's broadcast lectures of 1934, from which I have taken the title of this book, *A Commonsense View of all Music*.

The selection of the quotations which head each chapter was chosen from the synopsis of Grainger's 1934 lectures, and from his papers 'Collecting with the Phonograph' (1908) and 'The Impress of Personality in Unwritten Music' (1915). I picked out what seemed to me to be at the heart of Grainger's thinking and of most significance in the present state of ethnomusicology and music education. I paired six phrases and one general exhortation from Grainger's writings with topics that reflected my own interests and 'readings of Grainger's score'. The original lectures 3, 4 and 5 were dominated by a wide range of musical examples, and were intended to provide the sort of evidence on which the principles of the first two discursive lectures and the practical applications of the last two were based. The attempt to strike a balance between verbal discourse and listening to music has not been repeated in this book, though.

The first two chapters concentrate on fundamental discoveries of ethnomusicological research which Grainger repeatedly stressed: the complexity of unwritten, 'folk' music, and the individuality and creative imagination of its composers and performers. It was wrongly thought, and still is in some quarters, that music had progressed from 'simple' to 'complex', and that the 'simple' musics of non-literate peoples were the products of musical collectives rather than the work of individual composers and composer-performers. My own reflections on these topics touch on the problems of evolution and 'progress' in music, the role of individuals in musical and general cultural change, and the significance of different kinds of *activity* (such as music-making) in human decision-making and social organization. I argue that Percy Grainger implicitly, and sometimes directly, claimed that musicality is a basic ingredient of human nature and that artistic praxis is not only the best means for individual personal development, but the most efficient and potent source of human intellectual and cultural life in general.

The next three chapters address the variety of musical ideas, and of their different sources, which is revealed by a study of world musics. Percy Grainger felt that this alone was sufficient reason for including them in all music education. He found three features to be particularly characteristic of 'unwritten music': 'irregular' rhythmic patterns, 'lovely' melodies, and 'democratic' polyphony. In emphasizing their cognitive, affective, and social sources in chapters 3, 4 and 5 respectively, I have tried to explore further Grainger's notion that life reflects art, rather than vice versa, and to point the way to identifying an innate, pre-linguistic mode of human thought which could be called 'musical'.

Chapters 6 and 7 are concerned with applying the discoveries of ethnomusicology, especially in music education. Grainger's thoughts on the sensitizing role of music in life and on the range of musics that should be used are timely, as musical perform-ances are being increasingly used to assert national or ethnic identity and cultural hegemony, as the gaps between professional and amateur are growing wider, and as musical experience is being entrenched as a pleasant leisure activity rather than a central feature of human labour and intellectual life.

This book was designed to be a tribute to Percy Grainger as a pioneer in the fields of ethnomusicology and music education, but as such it is inevitably inadequate. It was for Grainger an article of faith that people should *listen* to all kinds of music and be allowed to respond to its beauty and spiritual message with their own innate musicality and aesthetic preferences, and without the interference of words and cultural chauvinism. Though many of the examples which I played in the original lectures were from my own tape collection, there are enough published recordings of world music to obviate the need for a special accompanying tape or disc, with all the complications of copyright and the extra expense of production. Percy Grainger's own choice of music is given in Appendix A, and in the 'Notes on recordings' (p. 194) I have listed some useful collections and specific recordings that relate to the text.

Similarly, I have not provided musical transcriptions, since even an exceptionally accurate score, such as Percy Grainger's in Appendix B, does not convey the reality of performance to someone who is not acquainted with the *sounds* of the music. Besides, I have come increasingly to doubt the merits of printing transcriptions of music of different cultural traditions without accompanying recordings that reveal their incompleteness: transcriptions can too easily be divorced from the reality of performance in context, and the structure and meaning of the music that they portray can be grossly distorted in the cause of some academic enterprise. I have, therefore, included only a very few musical illustrations as diagrams rather than as representations of the actual sounds of music.

The quotations from Grainger's writings are accompanied by page references from Teresa Balough's (1982) centenary collection of his work, which is more easily accessible than the originals. Similarly, Erica Mugglestone's (1982) translation of Guido Adler's paper of 1885 and Warren Dwight Allen's (1962) book are used for some references to evolutionary approaches to music history.

Specific acknowledgements are given at the end of this section for permission to use quotations and illustrations. It remains to thank those who contributed in many ways to the production of this book, but who should not be held responsible for any of its deficiencies. I am particularly grateful to my hosts at the University of Western Australia, and especially to Frank and Kathleen Callaway, Basil and Dianne Sansom, David and Paula Tunley, and Margaret Seares, who kindly shared her office with me. I thank also Wendy Trivett, Joanne Curtis, and Sharon Fryer for secretarial assistance, and Nancy McKenzie for typing the original lecture scripts, and Elspeth Larkin for typing the revised version.

I am grateful to Rosemary Dooley for support and advice when the manuscript was first considered for publication, and to Penny Souster for her patience and for many valuable comments during an elephantine period of gestation. Finally, I thank Zureena, Leila, Thalia and Munira for their love and their indulgence of my frequent abstraction and absence.

Acknowledgements

I am most grateful to Dr Teresa Balough for permission to include several quotations and material from the volume on Percy Grainger which she edited, *A musical genius from Australia* (1982); to Professor Nicholas England and Dr Ankica Petrović for permission to reproduce transcriptions on pp. 11–12 and 16–18 respectively; and to Mr Stewart Manville for permission to reprint the synopsis of Grainger's broadcast lectures in Appendix A.

1

'The complexity of folk music': evolution, invention and diffusion in music

ETHNOMUSICOLOGY AND FOLK MUSIC

Percy Grainger's contributions to ethnomusicology and music education are rarely mentioned in the same breath as those of his illustrious contemporaries Bartók and Kodály, although his feeling for folk music and musicians and his conception of the scope of music education were in some respects broader and more perceptive. This is partly because his published output was smaller, and partly because he allowed his eccentricities to overshadow the basic seriousness of his work and his outlook. If he had devoted as much time and energy to ethnomusicology and music education as did Bartók and Kodály, and if the continental foundations of his musical education in Frankfurt had not been undermined by English dilettantism and the disastrous influence of his mother (see Bird 1982: 176), I am sure that his ultimate contribution to the world of music would have been much greater.

Percy Grainger's major ethnomusicological papers on 'Collecting with the Phonograph' (1908) and 'The Impress of Personality in Unwritten Music' (1915) set standards of fieldwork and musical transcription which were rarely equalled in the 1950s and 1960s, and which even in the 1980s are not always accepted as minimum requirements. His own creativity, intuition, and sensitivity to the musicianship of other people helped him to understand what is too often forgotten in discussions and performances of unwritten music, namely, that a folk music tradition is not the product of some amorphous ethnic collective, and that musical sensitivity is neither acquired by being born a member of a particular group nor limited to appreciating the musical conventions of that group. Just as people do not acquire

1

Englishness or Irishness (whatever those concepts might mean) simply by being brought up in the homes of English or Irish parents, or in communities of English or Irish people, so people's musicality and musical interests are not entirely determined by their environment and social background. In re-working musical material, composers and performers have used current artistic conventions and have often been influenced by other members of their communities; but their production of music has always been the result of individual choice and of using certain processes of making musical sense of the world.

Folk music, no less than the so-called 'art music' of Asia and Europe, has been composed by individuals and continually re-composed by individual performers. It is precisely because of this that musical innovations have been possible and musical tra-ditions can be maintained, and that the aesthetic force of music can influence social action in other spheres. If music-making lacked any agreed conventions, it could not be effective as a means of communication; but if those conventions were to determine all individual expression, and if music-making were to be a mere routine that reflected extra-musical values and enshrined 'ethnic' identity, it could not be a dynamic factor in human society. The widely used label of 'ethnic' music implictly denies the existence of the individual creative impulse, which has enabled people throughout history and in all parts of the world to produce infinite varieties of beautiful music. Percy Grainger hoped that knowledge and appreciation of this variety would become commonplace, so that music might become a universal language. In a broadcast over Radio WEVD, in New York, on 20 June 1933, he concluded:

I firmly believe that music will someday become a 'universal language'. But it will not become so as long as our musical vision is limited to the output of 4 European countries between 1700 and 1900. The first step in the right direction is to view the music of all peoples and periods without prejudice of any kind, and to strive to put the world's known and available best music INTO CIRCULATION. Only then shall we be justified in calling music a 'universal language'.   (Balough 1982:113)

The situation has improved greatly since Grainger spoke those words, but progress has not been comparable to progress in science, medicine, and engineering. It has, perhaps, been a little better than progress in politics during the past fifty years – which is not really saying very much. A larger percentage of people listens to the music of Dufay and of contemporary composers, and to the musics of Africa, Asia, and Latin America, and great strides forward have been made in some music departments in Australia and the USA, and more recently in Europe. But Grainger's idea of music as a universal language is still a vision of the future, and we continue to live in a world in which people's musical experience reflects divisions of wealth, creed, class and nation which breed poverty, ignorance and violence.

I am convinced that Grainger's plan is feasible, and that it can best be brought about by developments in music education and ethnomusicology. I regard ethnomusicology as a method, rather than an area of study. It is not simply concerned with the study of so-called 'folk', 'primitive', and 'popular' musics, and the 'art' musics of Asia. It is not simply comparative musicology, in which exotic musical systems are analysed in relation to the parameters of the European tonal system and with the pseudo-scientific yard-sticks of the acoustical properties of sound and human musicality as measured by culture-specific tests. It is rather an approach to understanding *all* musics and music-making in the contexts of performance and of the ideas and skills that composers, performers and listeners bring to what they define as musical situations. One of the first lessons that ethnomusicologists learn is that music is both a social fact and multi-media communication: there are many societies that have no word for 'music' and do not isolate it conceptually from dance, drama, ritual, or costume; and even when music is identified as a specific category of thought and action, there are many different ways in which it is defined and in which different characteristics are regarded as significant.

Although the Greeks classified foreigners as *barbaroi* on the grounds that their speech was unintelligible, at least they were able to recognize that those people spoke languages. The same cannot be said for musics. Ethnomusicologists have not yet found a society without behaviour that they could define as 'musical'; but there are many societies and individuals who really cannot identify some other people's music as music when they hear it. Because there are so many different perceptions and conceptual-izations of music, it is necessary to approach the music-making of any individual human being in relation to several different 'worlds of music'.

These worlds of music can be usefully envisaged as areas within a series of concentric circles. First, there is the unknown world of music which composers, performers and listeners want to explore as much as ethnomusicologists. Are all musics human inventions, based on the application of general cognitive and motor skills? Or are they attempts to reify and understand better some special, innate capacity and biological force that all human bodies possess? Do we have music because some individuals invented it at a particular moment of human history, or are we human beings because we are 'musical'? And how does our musical experience relate to the world of nature, and to what has been called 'the music of the spheres'?

Secondly, there are the worlds of music that are identified as different musical systems by ethnomusicologists. Thirdly, there are the worlds of the social and cultural systems in which musical activity takes place. Fourthly, there are the worlds of music which exist as traditions or cultural systems within and across the broader worlds of different societies and cultures. Fifthly, there are the different worlds of music that individuals create: a composer's style, a performer's repertoire, and a listener's preferences. Although these different worlds of music are inter-related, they are not hierarchically dependent. For example, an individual composer is not necessarily a microcosm or reflection of a society or its prevalent musical system. Sibelius may have been a national and even a nationalist composer; but an understanding of Finnish society and culture and of the late-nineteenth-century European musical tradition will not go very far to explain the extraordinary originality and impact of his Seventh Symphony.

Although ethnomusicology must be concerned with *all* worlds of music if it is to produce a valid theory of human musical behaviour, its methodology has been developed through the study of the so-called 'art' musics of Asia and 'folk' musics of the world. It was the latter which captured the imagination of Percy Grainger when he came to Europe at the turn of this century. He was, in fact, an ethnomusicologist long before the term was coined by Jaap Kunst around 1950, and his work was a fine model for researchers. A great deal of contemporary fieldwork and analysis in ethnomusicology would be better if his advice was followed more carefully.

In 1908, *The Journal of the Folk Song Society* published his remarkable article on 'Collecting with the Phonograph'. Apart from setting a standard for transcription that has too often been ignored, and making several practical suggestions, which have periodically been 'rediscovered', Grainger foresaw the enormous importance of analyses of recorded performances in context, which only began to become accepted as a principle of ethnomusicological research in the 1960s. He foresaw too the need for what emerged as the Seeger Melograph (cf. Seeger 1957, 1958). Of the accuracy of his transcriptions (see Appendix B) A.L. Lloyd wrote in 1967:

the folk singer would convey the mood of the song by a small alteration of pace, a slight change of vocal timbre, an almost imperceptible pressing or lightening of rhythm, and by nuances of ornament that our folklorists, with the exception of Percy Grainger, have consistently neglected in their transcriptions.   (Lloyd 1967:78)

Grainger's stated desire for graphic displays of music, and for other scientific inventions to supplement the gramophone and phonograph, was stimulated by his concern to demonstrate 'the complexity of folk music' and 'the impress of personality in unwritten music'. Critics of the Melograph, who argue that a machine cannot help us to understand the essentially human qualities and meanings of music, should read Grainger. He leaves us in no doubt that he wants to use scientific methods for humanist aims. We need scientific aids to reveal the complexities of unwritten music because, as he also wrote in 1915, 'primitive music is too complex for untrained modern ears' (Balough 1982:65). Making transcriptions from recordings of folk music refines and sharpens our ears, and an additional visual display can help us to listen harder to what we hear, just as the visual stimulus of an orchestral score can help us to listen to passages whose importance might otherwise escape us.

Grainger pointed out that in the performance of folk-singers,

Rhythmical irregularities of every kind are everywhere in evidence, and the folk-scales in which their so-called 'modal' melodies move are not finally fixed as are our art-scales, but abound with quickly alternating major and minor thirds, sharp and flat sevenths, and (more rarely) major and minor sixths, and whereas the sixth of the scale occurs usually merely as a passing note all the other intervals are attacked freely, either jumpingly from one to the other, or as initial notes in phrases.   (Balough 1982:70)

'Grainger's ultimate goal in collecting, transcribing and arranging folkmusic was to make the world's music available to the world. He worked in the hope that people would grow to become more aware of the beauties of the musical achievements of all races and cultures of the world, thus helping to engender human understanding' (Balough 1982:18). His anxiety about the disappearance of musical treasures led him to concentrate on collecting and transcribing unwritten, or so-called 'folk' music, music that was aurally transmitted and whose structural principles were carried in the heads of the performers and their audiences. His approach was practical, but his imagination and insight, and the thoroughness of his methods, put him in an entirely different league from most contemporary collectors of unwritten music. His ideas were very much in tune with modern ethnomusicology.

Most significantly for us today, he was one of the first to undermine the mistaken notion that music had progressed from simple to complex, and that unwritten music was a survival from the prehistoric past.

To appreciate the originality of Grainger's approach, we need to know something of the views of music and music history which held sway at the turn of the century, and particularly the dominance of ideas of evolution and progress.

CONCEPTS OF EVOLUTION AND PROGRESS IN MUSIC HISTORY

Much writing in historical musicology has claimed implicitly or explicitly that the evolution of the musical art has been furthered by the invention of musicians of genius, whose ideas and work have been diffused by performance, by music education, or by economic and colonial expansion, to wherever the art of music was practised. The concept of evolution generally used was not derived from the biological evolution of Charles Darwin, who had insisted that the idea of evolution must not be equated with the current Victorian notion of a drive to perfection, and had warned in his letters, 'Never use the words higher and lower'. It was derived more from the idea of evolution as an organic historical process from homogeneous to heterogeneous, which had been proposed chiefly by Herbert Spencer. Thus in 1885, Guido Adler wrote:

How starting from the beginnings of simple melody the structure of works of art grows by degrees, how proceeding from the simplest postulates the artistic norms latent in the production of sound become more and more complicated, how sound systems vanish with disappearing cultures, how a series of cells gradually attaches itself to the limb and so grows organically, how elements which stand outside the movement of progress become extinct because not viable – to demonstrate and trace these principles is the most profitable exercise of the scholar in the arts.   (Mugglestone 1982:8)

These ideas influenced musical scholarship for many years to come, and Adler never changed his mind. In 1924, he reiterated that 'the task of music history is the research in and presentation of the products of musical thought in the processes of evolution'. The interesting question is how such a varied collection of ideas about social, intellectual, and biological evolution could have held sway for so long.

Hindemith is one of several composers who have argued that works of art are conceived as wholes, 'in the flash of a single moment' (Hindemith 1953:61), and that the details, the 'simple melodies', often come last in the creative process. There is plenty of evidence that 'artistic norms latent in the production of sound' do *not* become more and more complicated, and that sound systems do *not* vanish with disappearing cultures (witness Afro-American music). The organic analogy for processes of diffusion is unhelpful, and the ethnocentric theory of the march of progress has been successfully refuted by the activities of many of the oppressed and so-called 'backward' peoples of the world. Dahlhaus (1983:14–18) has summarized the arguments against Adler's use of the organic model, which he had elaborated in his theory of musical style.

Perhaps Adler's influence derived chiefly from his proposal of a system at a time when a coherent sense of direction was needed, and also from the contemporary interest in ideas of progress and social evolution. Spencer's theory of evolution from homogeneous to heterogeneous, Helmholtz's research on the sensations of tone and the laws of the constitution of musical sound, and the early discoveries of so-called 'primitive' musics in some of the colonial outposts of the world, all seemed to come together towards the end of the nineteenth century to confirm and make more 'scientific' earlier writings on music theory, and to explain the course that Western music had taken since the Middle Ages.

This quasi-'scientific' quest for an all-embracing theory led to histories of music that were full of speculations about music that the authors had never heard or could not possibly have heard. Thus, in 1861, Ambros declared that the music of Babylon 'was quite certainly voluptuous and noisy', and Phoenician music was mainly meant to drown 'the cries of the victims who burned in the glowing arms of Moloch'. This perpetuated the attitude of Krause, who in 1827 had written: 'In Antiquity, which was the childhood of music, only simple unadorned melody was known, as is the case today with such peoples as the Hindus, Chinese, Persians and Arabs, who have not yet progressed beyond the childhood age' (cf. Sachs 1961:7–8 and Allen 1962:92). These grand surveys of music history ignored what little empirical work had been done decades earlier, such as a study on Chinese music by Father Joseph Amiot in 1779, and three volumes on Egyptian music by Guillaume-André Villoteau in 1800, which were based on three and a half years of intensive fieldwork in Egypt.

1885 also marked the publication of John Frederic Rowbotham's book *A History of Music to the Time of the Troubadours*, in which he adopted Herbert Spencer's theory that music originated in an excess of nervous energy and in impassioned speech. He argued that the first and most important influence in changing from impassioned speech to vocal music was the story, which encouraged people to confine the voice to one note.

First, men were contented with one note...A long time must have elapsed before tone itself would come to be looked upon as a subject for objective treatment. The very first musical note ever heard in the world was G, and for a very long time indeed the whole musical art lay in embryo in that note. The living illustrations of the primitive period are those people who are generally looked upon as in the lowest stage of human development, the natives of Tierra del Fuego, etc.

(Allen 1962:111)

Rowbotham followed the fashionable anthropological method of treating contemporary 'primitive' music as a survival from the past, a kind of living fossil. One Fuegian song was quoted 'in which they get beyond their one note', and so could be seen as 'emerging from the one-note period in Music'. The Samoans were given as a living example of the two-note stage in musical history, and the evolution of music continued with three-, four- and five-note melodies, with suitable examples given for each stage. The concept of survivals ignored the uses of music in society, and the influence that use may have on musical structure. Thus in practice, one- and two-note music can be used for sophisticated rituals, as in Hawai'i or India, but the same people use more tones in other contexts.

There was another study of music history published in 1885 which was more sensitive to cultural factors. In his *Histoire de la musique depuis les temps anciens jusqu'à nos jours*, Félix Clément had insisted that there was a unity in the senses of all mankind, and that differences in musics depend on culture and civilization:

Musical art is sociable by nature; thus mutual influence and exchanges of ideas contribute to its progress, as to the progress of other forms of knowledge.

Music being of all the arts that in which imagination and feeling have the greatest part, *exterior influences play a prominent role in the direction of ideas and the conception of great works.*

(Allen 1962:121)

If German scholarship and concepts of academic merit had not predominated in Europe, or if Clément had produced a system comparable to Adler's, musicology might have taken a more interesting course during the subsequent decades. But Clément's ideas were not really taken to heart by musicologists until much later. Sir Charles Hubert Parry had at least argued in 1896 (in *The Evolution of the Art of Music*) that 'the biographical method of music history had been carried too far and that the enquiry should be directed not so much to the evolution of genius, which is individual, but to the evolution of the art as a whole' (Allen 1962:112). But his emphasis on the evolution of *the art* tended to concentrate attention on music almost as a phenomenon that has self-generating power, and to lean too heavily on the idea of progress from simple to complex, from folk song to symphony.

The 'evolutionary process in the musical art' was seen as a more or less independent, progressing body of knowledge, like technology. The main flaw in using this approach for music or any of the arts is obvious when one considers that a piece of old music is not like a vintage car or a Sopwith Camel or a Handley Page Hercules. It is always available-for-use as a viable part of contemporary life, and can always be assigned new, contemporary meanings.

Curiously enough, very much the same attitude to musical evolution was taken by Curt Sachs in his last book, *The Wellsprings of Music* (1961). Even though he modified some of the more rudimentary evolutionary schemes that he had proposed in earlier works, and insisted that simple to complex in musical structure does *not* necessarily imply any progress, he still wrote of 'palaeolithic stages' of music and 'palaeolithic survivals', and estimated the antiquity of music in terms of its music product. Instead of moving from one- to two- and three-tone melodies, he argued that the oldest music consists of 'tumbling strains' and 'one-note melodies'.

This was essentially the same procedure as that adopted by the other 'evolutionists' whom I have criticized. His attitude to the data is made clear by his equation of 'oldest music' with 'lowest cultural level'. His notion of cultural level was based primarily on the evidence of material culture, and seems to have ignored phenomena such as the highly complex kinship systems or cosmologies that accompany some technologically simple means of production.

According to Sachs's notion of cultural level, the !Kung 'Bushmen' and the Babinga 'Pygmies' present very serious problems. For they are hunter-gatherers, but they practise polyphony! (Cf. *Bushmen Music and Pygmy Music*, LP record LD9, published by the Peabody Museum, Harvard University, and the Département d'Ethnomusicologie, Musée de l'Homme, Paris.)

It may seem superfluous to spend so much time discussing an approach to music history that has been criticised fully in Warren Dwight Allen's *Philosophies of Music History* (1939, 2nd edition 1962), and which Sir Jack Westrup demolished with an elegance and economy that cannot be matched, in his book *An Introduction to Musical History* (1955, 2nd edition 1973). He reminded us that Purcell is not more complex than Byrd, and that 'continuity does not necessarily imply either continuous development from simple to complex, or progress from a lower to a higher level':

Exx. 1a–c   Three songs of the !Kung San of the Kalahari, Botswana.
Transcriptions by Dr Nicholas England (1967:63–4)

Ex. 1a   !Koa-Ts'i (Giraffe Song)

Ex. 1b   !Khari-Tsi (Quicken Song)

Ex. 1a Ŋǃŋ Ts'i-ma (Eland Song Little)

the terms 'simple' and 'complex' are often ambiguous and need precise definition before they can be applied satisfactorily to individual works of art. The idea that music progresses as it develops is even more illusory. Is eighteenth-century music 'better' than the music of the sixteenth century, is Vaughan Williams a 'better' composer than Beethoven? . . . There is no objection whatever to speaking of the 'evolution' of music, but we shall get into great difficulties if we regard it as synonymous with progress.   (Westrup 1973:13)

I have devoted time to a critical discussion of evolutionary approaches to music partly because nineteenth-century notions still persist, even among 'folk' music researchers and in the BBC's Radio 3, and partly because I want to reinstate the notion of evolution in understanding music and music-making, but this

cannot be done until it has been made clear that I am *not* trying
to revive Spencerian concepts of evolution.

As recently as 1965, Fritz Bose (1966:219) argued that 'the
study of the stratigraphy of primitive music is one of the most
important tasks of modern ethnomusicology'. And in 1978, I was
stunned to read a BBC poster announcing a series of programmes
on Radio 3: *Plainsong and the Rise of European Music*. The blurb
talked of 'the supremacy of Western music'; and it quoted in large
type from Dom Gregory Murray OSB:

Gregorian chant constitutes the greatest body of pure melody in existence . . . it lies at the foundation of all Western music.

There are many educated Japanese, Chinese, Indians and
Javanese, and even some Americans brought up in Western
schools of music, who could not agree that Western European
music is supreme above all other systems. There are scholars of
Persian and Arabic music who would question the claim of
Gregorian chant to be 'the greatest body of pure melody in
existence'. It is doubtful, too, if Gregorian chant really was the
foundation of all Western music. Although much early European
polyphony was not so much 'a different kind of musical technique' as 'an embellishment of the single monophonic line,
usually built on a plainsong stem', what made that development
possible was the intrusion of dance, 'the prototype of all
measured music . . . if the singers were to keep together mensuration became inevitable. Basically the change from monody to
polyphony was not a harmonic but a rhythmic one' (Mellers
1950:49–50). Similarly, later developments in Western music
derived more from the folk songs and dance music that inspired
Luther, Haydn, Mozart, Beethoven, Schubert, and many other
composers.

The implication that there was, or even has been, a unilinear
evolution of music, that there is one foundation rather than
many, ignores the complex class structures of the societies of
which the so-called Western European musical system was a part.
It ignores the facts that this system was practised by only a
minority of the population, and that when different groups came
to power, they often brought with them the music of their class,
which may well have sprung from different foundations.

THE VARIETIES OF MUSICAL INVENTION

I have emphasized that a musical tradition can have multiple foundations, or what Gilbert Chase (1976) called 'a multitude of continuities'. It is also important to remember that music can be produced by a variety of processes, not all of which are directly concerned with the organization of 'forms in tonal motion', to paraphrase Eduard Hanslick (cf. Blacking 1973:12–21).

This was the central theme of another publication that appeared in 1885 along with the work of Guido Adler, Félix Clément, and Frederic Rowbotham. Alexander John Ellis was an English physicist who was concerned, amongst other things, to promote, and then to test and challenge the arguments of Helmholtz. He has been called 'the father of ethnomusicology' because of his paper 'On the musical scales of various nations', but the implications of his argument were not generally appreciated or followed up until well into the twentieth century. And even today, over a hundred years after his paper appeared, his insights have not become a part of our musical pedagogy. The significance of his paper is not even mentioned in *The New Grove*.

What Ellis asserted was that musical tones are social facts. After measuring the scales of different musical systems, he concluded:

> The musical scale is not one, not 'natural', nor even founded necessarily on the laws of the constitution of musical sound so beautifully worked out by Helmholtz, but very diverse, very artificial, and very capricious.
> (Ellis 1885:526)

Ellis's work stressed the importance of invention in music and the individuality of cultural systems as modes of thought. His conclusions should have shattered the evolutionary framework, but the impact of his study was not to be felt for many years, and even some ethnomusicologists still analyse musical systems independently of the cultural systems in which they are embedded.

When we look at music in Ellis's terms, rather than the terms defined by Guido Adler, then we can see more clearly the relationships between some 'folk' music systems and music that is composed for 'performance' by means of a computer. Like the music of the !Kung San or the ancient Chinese, computer music is the sonic result of humanly organized symbols. Though it eliminates live performance, computer music is conceptually a performing art. Moreover, computer composers may have something to learn from music systems whose principles of order are conceived in general symbolic, rather than specifically sonic, terms. Throughout the world, composers adopt different techniques, from hearing sounds in their head, out of which they want to create order, to having a vision of order that can be transformed into sound. It is remarkable how the coherence and consistency of musical compositions that are conceived without direct reference to their sound structures, can be deeply affecting, as if human beings are touched by the immanence of a beautiful structure, although they hear only the resultant sounds. And so the message of 'folk' musicians to computer composers might be: 'Don't worry too much about the sounds you want to make; think about the numerical symbols with which a computer can produce sounds, and invent humanly significant order with them.'

It is not only computer music that has its parallels in systems of unwritten music, and that was why Percy Grainger insisted that contemporary composers had many lessons to learn from them. In 1915 he wrote (*Musical Quarterly* of July): 'modern geniuses and primitive music unite in teaching us the charm of "wrong notes that sound right"'. Indeed, chords of major and minor seconds that would be considered discordant in terms of acoustical theories of musical structure, were regarded as harmonious by the mountain people of Bosnia and Herzegovina whose two-part *ganga* songs were studied by Dr Ankica Petrović. This was enhanced by the way in which they were performed: singers stood very close to each other, and the vibrations from the loudly sung, close intervals induced pleasant bodily sensations. Dr Florian Messner (1980) has described similar music which is performed in Europe, Asia, and as far east as Papua New Guinea. The German word *Schwebungsdiaphonie* expresses its form and character better than any English equivalent.

Dr Petrović's research also supported Grainger's argument that the subtleties of 'folk' music could escape the ears even of trained European musicians. Several writers on *ganga* had eliminated ornaments in their transcriptions of the singing, and had even 'polished up' the songs, on the grounds that they were attempts of musically uneducated peasants to imitate the polyphony of the art music that they would have heard in towns and country mansions. Dr Petrović demonstrated that *ganga* was a highly developed, consciously created genre with rules and regional styles that are recognized by all people in the area on the basis of their contrasting *musical* features, such as variations in ornament, in length of sections, or rules of two-part counterpoint.

Exx. 2a–c   Three *ganga* from different villages in Bosnia and Herzegovina. Transcriptions by Dr Ankica Petrović

Ex. 2a

Ex. 2b

Ex. 2c

She herself did not hear all these differences when she began her fieldwork, and she thought that people were talking about *social* parameters and their knowledge of *who* was singing. By careful transcriptions of recorded performances, and by playing recordings to villagers for identification, she found out that people made musical judgements and that their judgements were invariably right.

The musical competence of ordinary people has been further confirmed by Leon Crickmore's (1968) carefully researched analysis of musical appreciation, in which he found that music structures were comprehended independently of personality, measured intellectual capacity, and musical intelligence as assessed by the Wing test.

Small children show a remarkable ability to identify music and to sing, especially if they are in an environment that stimulates and encourages such capacities. Moreover, their abilities are by no means restricted to some kind of biological programming which requires that they graduate from two to seven tones by slow degrees. For example, when I was living with the Venda of Southern Africa between 1956 and 1958, children learnt to sing songs with 2, 3, 4, 5, 6 and 7 tones in a sequence that reflected the popularity of certain songs or their relevance in daily life; they had assimilated the principles of melodic and harmonic construction and could correct me when I was wrong; and by the age of eight or nine many children could set melodies to new words, thus showing that they had grasped the rules that related melodic line to changes in the patterns of speech-tone.

What figures frequently in the literature in ethnomusicology and once again confirms Grainger's arguments, is the importance of the creative process of making music, whether it be the invention of a piece by a composer, or its re-invention by performers and listeners. Every performance, or mental rehearsal of a performance, can be a creative experience for all concerned, because performers and audience alike must re-create it.

Specific music structures and ideas have been invented at given moments of time, but the musical process which gives life to those structures and ideas is constantly evolving – to such an extent that one might ask whether each single invention has any more significance than the imperceptible gaps between pitches which make a melody rather than a glissando. If Serkin, Solomon, Arrau, Ashkenazy, Barenboim, Kemp, and Pollini can transform the musical code of Beethoven's 'Hammerklavier' Sonata so differently, is there really such a phenomenon as *the Hammerklavier*? And which, if any, of these interpretations is Beethoven's? Surely there is some evolutionary significance in the fact that Horowitz's 1977 recording of Liszt's B minor Piano Sonata takes three minutes longer than the recording he made in 1932, even if the change reflects the evolution of Horowitz's body rather than of the society in which he lives. If it *is* the consequence of Horowitz's independent, personal evolution, the longer performance is certainly not the result of physical decay or a diminution of intentionality.

DIFFUSION AND INVENTION

The very survival of a performing arts tradition depends on its transmission from one person or group to another. And yet, from what I have said about the ubiquity of musical creativity and invention, it should be clear that the notion of 'tradition' is perhaps false. It evokes a static model of musical continuity, which does not relate to the dynamic reality of any musical performance whether of written or unwritten music. Just as considerable variations in performance do not disturb the notion of continuity in written music, so it would be wrong to think of unwritten, aurally transmitted music as haphazard or all improvised. It is carefully constructed and frequently rehearsed, and audiences are as aware of mistakes as they are of the details that make particular performances and the versions of some performers more attractive than others. Many societies distinguish between music that must be performed as 'correctly' as possible, such as Maori Waiata singing (cf. McLean 1978:27), and music that ought to be improvised or at least differ considerably from one performance to another. The reasons for these contrasts are usually to be found in the uses to which different kinds of music are put in a particular society.

The transmission of performance practice from one generation to another is a form of diffusion, though the term is more commonly used to refer to the spread of traits from one society to another. What I wish to emphasize is that whether music is diffused from one generation to another, as are certain traditions of pianistic skill, or from one society to another, as European music in parts of Africa, African music in the Americas, and Chinese music in Korea, the process of diffusion is invariably influenced more by the re-interpretation and re-invention of the receivers than the offerings of the givers. What is really puzzling is why people should want any continuity of expression in a performing art like music; and that problem takes us to the very roots of the musical language, with its emphasis on repetition and its high level of redundancy.

MUSIC IN THE CONTEXT OF BIOLOGICAL EVOLUTION

Percy Grainger's emphasis on the complexity of folk music and the potential musicality of ordinary people, and his belief in the value of widely differing kinds of music have been upheld by the work of ethnomusicologists. Attempts to trace the evolution of the musical art from simple to complex, from one-tone to twelve-tone music and beyond, and to fit all the music of the world into such schemes, have proved fruitless. Musical systems are derived neither from some universal emotional language nor from stages in the evolution of a musical art: they are made up of socially accepted patterns of sound that have been invented and developed by interacting individuals in the contexts of different social and cultural systems. If they have been diffused from one group to another, they have frequently been invested with new meanings and even new musical characteristics, because of the creative imagination of performers and listeners.

Role distinctions between creator, performer and listener, variations in musical styles and contrasts in the apparent musical ability of composers and performers, are consequences not of different genetic endowment, but of the division of labour in society, of the functional interrelationship of groups and of the commitment of individuals to music-making as a social activity. Distinctions between music as 'folk', 'art', or 'popular' reflect a concern with musical products, rather than with the dynamic processes of music-making.

Such distinctions tell us nothing substantive about different styles of music, and as categories of value they can be applied to all music. 'Popular' music as a general category of value, is music that is liked or admired by people in general, and it can include Bach, Beethoven, the Beatles, Ravi Shankar, Sousa's marches and the 'Londonderry Air'. Far from being a patronizing or derogatory term, it describes positively music that has succeeded in its basic aim to communicate as *music*. The music that most people value most is popular music; but what that music is varies according to the social class and experience of composers, performers and listeners. Similarly, as Grainger pointed out, 'folk' musicians strive for artistic perfection. As Eric Gill said, 'It isn't that artists are special kinds of people.

It's that people are special kinds of artists.' And so we could say that the goal of all folk is to make artistic popular music.

It can be argued that throughout human prehistory, and for at least ninety-three per cent of the time since the emergence of our species (*homo sapiens sapiens*) approximately 70,000 years ago, all music was popular in so far as it was shared and enjoyed by all members of a society. If there were distinctions of style within a society's music, they were probably accepted as signs of functional or social differentiation rather than as barriers to mutual communication. There is evidence that early human species were able to dance and sing several hundred thousand years before *homo sapiens sapiens* emerged with the capacity for speech as we now know it (see Livingstone 1973, Blacking 1976).

It is unlikely that the antiquity of music can ever be proved. The arguments can only be supported by inferences from our knowledge of contemporary brain function and from study of early human skeletal remains, and from the evidence of universal musicality among many of the societies whose musical practices have been studied by folklorists, anthropologists and ethnomusicologists. It would be quite wrong, though, to regard any contemporary society of hunter-gatherers or horticulturalists as a survival of palaeolithic or early neolithic times: nearly 10,000 years of history and constant social change separate the Aurignacians and Magdalenians of prehistoric Europe from the San of the Kalahari Desert or the Aranda of Central Australia. Nevertheless, the study of music-making in small-scale societies with a minimal division of labour has suggested that capacities for music are species-specific; that the forms that the art takes are influenced by the structure of the brain and by the patterns of the cultural systems in which their creators are reared; and that this evidence is sufficient to justify some inferences about music-making in all human societies, past and present.

The invention of music is part of the process of *biological* evolution, that is, evolution in the Darwinian sense. The constraints and proclivities that affect the behaviour of the body influence the invention of culture, just as the intentionality of individual organisms influences animal behaviour and the course of evolution. History is not necessarily evolution: in fact, the course of events can be positively anti-evolutionary and suicidal, just as some societies can develop pathological cultures. This does not mean that culture is superorganic or that history is free of the pressures of evolution, but it does suggest that there are limits to human invention, and that if people depart too far from behaviour that is in the interest of the species as a whole, they endanger themselves, if not the whole species.

Though the material products of a society's culture may survive the extinction of the society and be given new meanings in the context of another culture, as are, for instance, objects in a museum, a culture itself survives only as long as people use it. A culture is always being invented and re-invented by individual decision-making, and although it may give the impression of being more permanent than the individuals who constitute it, and cultural evolution has depended on the accumulation of knowledge and the expansion of societies, it is really humanity that is permanent and constantly evolving, and culture that is transient and dependent on human whim.

Music expresses these contradictions of the human condition most faithfully. As a metaphor of feeling 'that can reveal the nature of feelings with a detail and truth that language cannot approach' (Langer 1948:191), it expresses the state of human nature in the context of different cultures. Its structures reflect the replication and repetition of ideas and sequences of action and the need to share sentiments and concepts, which are essential features of *culture*, while the obligation to remake music at every performance, and the possibility that it may be felt anew inside each individual body, reflect the evolutionary condition of *nature* that an organism, to survive, should constantly adapt to its changing environment.

The extension of the capacity for culture and the development of technological mastery have depended on human abilities to halt or control natural change. Music therefore obeys the laws of culture, and so through the bodily experiences that it induces enables human beings to come to terms with the natural *and* cultural grounds of their being: it is a kind of adaptive ritual behaviour that by the special nature of its means of production combines the creative conditions of objective technological mastery and subjective human experience.

In so far as music-making is a technique of the body that by repetition can halt change in a predictable way and transcend time and place, but only for as long as its makers are involved and experiencing it, it has special expressive power that routine technological processes lack. This is why musical evolution and invention cannot be described as progressive in the same way as technological developments. Each apparently new idea in music 'does not really grow out of previously expressed ideas, though it may well be limited by them'. It is a new emphasis that grows out of composers' experiences of their environments, 'a realization of certain aspects of the experience available to all human beings which seem' to them 'to be particularly relevant in the light of contemporary events and personal experiences' (Blacking 1973:72–3).

The role of music as mediator between nature and culture, between evolution and invention, explains apparent contradictions in its appreciation, as well as the conditions of creation and performance. Those who enjoy the art that most successfully freezes time constantly demand that it move with the times. People expect a musical masterpiece to bring more delight on closer acquaintance and with repeated hearings, but at the same time demand that every new composition shall be different from its predecessors.

There is no problem about this apparent contradiction once it is appreciated that what is important about music is the special nature of the *musical event*, whether it be the novel production of a known work or the 're-production' of a novel work.

This emphasis on the musical event is familiar to those who specialize in the study of aurally transmitted music traditions, and it reminds us that music, like dance and drama, cannot exist without living people. Music must constantly be re-invented, and the participatory act of re-creation by performers and audience is as important a part of musical experience as the special form that their sequences of action take once they have agreed to make music.

Music is like many of the paintings and sculptures of traditional African societies: the art was in the making rather than in the finished piece. The labour of love was what mattered and what uplifted human beings, and the subsequent fate of its product was comparatively unimportant. The intricate body-paintings of the Nuba were washed off after a ritual; and I have seen women of the Nsenga of Zambia spend over two hours making a beautiful sculpture on the ground for a girls' initiation ritual, knowing that it would be destroyed in two minutes when the young novices danced on it. Similarly, there is nothing left after a musical performance except the memory, and perhaps the retention, of feelings.

An 'art object' by itself is neither art nor non-art: it only becomes one or the other because of the attitudes of human beings towards it. That is why there is nothing contradictory about the facts that an African craftsman can carve a stool with the same outlook as a factory-hand making mass-produced chairs, whilst European and American art-lovers come along and treat his stool as art. As an object, a painting or sculpture, or the score of a piece of music, may have objective reality, but as a work of *art* it cannot have such objective reality. Art lives *in* men and women, to be brought out into the open by special processes of interaction.

In the art and music of sub-Saharan Africa, in the people's systems of kinship and political organization, and in their philosophies and religious rituals, the emphasis was, and is, very much on feeling and process, with a sense of order derived from within the collective consciousness of the community and from nature. There are two important premises: first, communion between people is seen *not* as the result of a unique historical event, in which individual organisms made a rational decision to co-operate in production, but as an essential feature of the biologically inherited capabilities of the species. We are born social. Our species is not human, but human-and-fellow-human.

muthu ndi muthu nga vhanwe (Venda)
Umuntu ungumuntu ngabantu (Zulu)
A human being becomes human through other human beings.

The second premise is related to the first: activities which might be described as ritual, aesthetic, or artistic, are seen *not* merely as part of the superstructure of human social life, but as fundamental to intellectual and social life, and as integral parts of the process of production. In other words, certain kinds of non-profit-making activity are seen as indispensable means to making a profit, and a great deal of time and effort is allocated to them. It follows, of course, from the first premise, that all notion of profit is seen ultimately in terms of the good of the community and the environment. The very condition of individual self-realization is sharing with others, just as a healthy community depends on the creative contribution of its individual members. Individuality in community is as important as a community of individuals. Life is an evolutionay process of becoming, in which individual consciousness is nurtured through collective experience and hence becomes the source of richer cultural forms.

Consider these African drum patterns both as experiences of becoming and as sources of richer cultural forms.

Exx. 3a–c   African drum patterns

These elementary musical exercises show how social interaction can be organized in such a way that feeling and intellect combine to create both a special social process and a new cultural product. Through musical interaction, two people create forms that are greater than the sum of their parts, and make for themselves experiences of empathy that would be unlikely to occur in ordinary social intercourse.

This example leads on to the topic of the second chapter,

'The Impress of Personality in Unwritten Music'. The sharing of ideas and feelings is fundamental to the process of becoming human, and we need to know what roles music has played and can play in that process.

2

'The Impress of Personality in Unwritten Music': music as a means of communication and ethnomusicology as social science

At the end of Ken Russell's television film on Sir Edward Elgar, the ailing composer lies opposite a window that looks towards Worcester Cathedral, and plays records of his own compositions on a clockwork HMV Model 163 gramophone by his bedside. Although the music of this very English composer had been first appreciated by German audiences, on this occasion its 'language' was scarcely English, let alone international. Its meaning was intensely private, recalling for the composer alone the musical and non-musical experiences that had inspired it. The very personal nature of musical composition and appreciation raises doubts that music can communicate knowledge and experience in the same ways that the meaning of a verbal statement can be commonly understood.

And yet Elgar expected others to share and understand the musical expression of his individual experience, and was disappointed when they did not. His love of the English countryside, his Catholicism, and his patriotism, were sentiments that involved others, and music was the means he chose to communicate his view of those sentiments. Even when people seemed to receive his musical message, they often missed its essential meaning: he was disgusted by the vulgarity and noise that passed for pomp and circumstance at the British Empire Exhibition of 1924, and *his* concept of a land of hope and glory was far removed from that of many who loved and will continue to be stirred by his magnificent melody: he envisaged groups of human beings joined in common enterprises that inspire fellowship, stretch their capacities, and nurture their sensibilities.

28

Elgar was clearly concerned with what music could do to people, and in this he was subscribing to a view of music that is surely centuries older than the myth of Orpheus. The conviction that music can transform experience, heighten consciousness, induce ecstasy, or even cure sickness, is perhaps universally held, and is a stimulus to countless musical performances. Although heightened experience or altered states of consciousness are not qualities peculiar to music, music has advantages over many other ways of heightening human experience, because of the special relationships between people and the kind of co-ordination of the body that are often required for performance.

Elgar knew well that the prolonged concentration of attention and sensitive interaction required for performance of the chamber music that he played with and wrote for his family and friends had a humanizing effect on all involved. His five years as band-master of the County Lunatic Asylum also taught him how music could transform the quality of life of the inmates with whom he worked. Similarly, anyone who has played in an African drum or pipe ensemble, where each performer provides only a small part of the total musical pattern, knows that special bodily experiences and relationships with other people are thrust on them by the requirements of the music: to produce the correct polyrhythmic and polyphonic patterns each player must maintain and relate his/her own inner tempo to that of others. In this way, the power of well-performed music can be related to the power that is generated by the extension of individuality in community.

Elgar also knew that just as the music of his *Enigma Variations* was stimulated by the memory of people and events in his personal life, so the personal response of others to his music would be influenced by the several channels of communication that must accompany any performance. As a metaphorical expression of feeling that is primarily sensuous and non-referential, music offers 'a representation of knowable facts, characteristic not of objective experience but of our consciousness of objective experience' (Ferguson 1960:88). Similarly our consciousness and comprehension of music is affected by other channels of communication that accompany it – even in a concert hall that is ostensibly devoted solely to musical communication. Who will deny that the gestures of conductors and soloists are important, or that encounters in the foyer, the tuning-up of the orchestra, the costumes of the audience, and the architecture and décor of the concert hall, supplement the communication of 'form in tonal motion'?

This is why the results of music association tests are always inconclusive, and why, after 'thousands of specimens from the music of all countries and all centuries' had been 'listened to and evaluated', it was found that 'when there are no words to give help, there are as many different meanings for the same musical messages, as there are different people' (Silbermann 1963:67–8). When tests are administered to subjects in artificial settings never envisaged by the creators of the music, how can the sounds, divorced from their social and cultural environment, be expected to communicate with any consistency, even when listeners belong to the same social class and agree broadly on certain principles of musical communication?

In *La musique et la transe* (1980), Gilbert Rouget dismissed Andrew Neher's laboratory experiments which purported to show that certain tempi of drumming would induce trance-like states: if there were inevitable physiological responses to music, 'the whole of sub-Saharan Africa would be in trance from the beginning to the end of the year' (Rouget 1977:234). Music can communicate nothing to unprepared and unreceptive minds, in spite of what some writers have suggested to the contrary.

The power of music *as music* must depend in the last resort on people's perceptions of specific patterns of melody, rhythm and texture, and on the bodily sensations and responses that these elicit. But in making sense of music, we are also influenced by other communications that reach our senses, by the social experiences that performance can evoke or actually requires, and especially by the quasi-ritual association and concentration of human bodies in time and space and the varying degrees of intensity and energy generated by the performers as participants in a social situation. In many cases, the use of music as a symbolic focus of attention and social interaction is more significant than any of its intrinsically musical characteristics.

These two aspects of musical communication, which we may call the musical and the social, need not be mutually exclusive: people use music, and music uses people. Moreover, people do things with music and music can do things to people. But in both cases (that is, if people are turned on either by music or by a social situation) what happens to them is possible only through some kind of resonance which has not been, and cannot easily be, proved.

The possibility of some special kind of musical sensitivity has greatly concerned composers and performers, and it is, in fact, the only real basis for a useful theory of musical communication. If human beings can never really share feelings, music must remain one of many cultural artefacts whose forms and effects are consequences of social and cultural convention or the idio-syncratic choice of individuals. If music communicates only in so far as individuals choose to listen to it or use it, and not necessarily with any regard to its intrinsically musical character-istics, there are no good musical reasons why two people should be expected to respond to Elgar's music in the same way, or in the way that he did. Music becomes a commodity that can be taken up or abandoned for an unlimited number of purposes, most of which probably have little or nothing to do with music.

This view of music was implied by the widely held, individu-alistic theory of musical creation and evolution which I discussed in my last chapter, but the consequences and inherent contra-dictions of this view are generally ignored. A mode of criticism that seeks to elevate the art of music and applaud its greatest exponents only succeeds in reducing music to a political gimmick and its exponents to performing chimpanzees, because it ignores the sensibility of ordinary listeners, those very capabilities that Elgar wanted to spark off in his fellow Englishmen. It is contra-dictory to exalt individuality in some people while denying it to the majority, unless it is done as part of a system of social control.

Thus, if the individuality of experience and uniqueness of a 'great' composer are stressed, but the listeners' individuality of perception is denied, the popularity of that composer or of one of his compositions cannot be explained in terms of his music and it need not have anything to do with *musical* communi-cation: it may as well be the result of a chance coincidence of different individual interests, of mass hysteria or hypnotism, or of successful propaganda or advertising. The logical consequence of such a view is far removed from the intentions of its promoters: it is simply that we should not waste more time studying the music of Bach, Beethoven, and other 'universally' popular composers, but concentrate on the social and political conditions and the means by which others are persuaded to endorse them as symbols of something *non*-musical. This is certainly an important aspect of the sociology of music, but I find it less interesting than the study of *musical* communication, because it is neither peculiar to music, nor about communication as a process of *sharing* knowledge and experience.

What is most interesting about Elgar's music is where and how his personal vision expressed something that could be truly shared with others. Elgar was as biologically unique as any other individual, and yet another human organism subjected to similar social and cultural experiences would possibly have produced similar results. If, at birth, the baby Elgar had been exchanged for the baby Mahler, or Richard Strauss, or Lloyd George, or Erich Ludendorff, the 'biological' Elgar might well have become one of these contemporaries, or they have become Elgar.

People do not automatically develop as individuals because of unique genetic endowment: individuality is the result of the discovery and development of the self in community in a series of circumstances and encounters whose sum is unique for each person. Individuality is a consequence of sharing with others, in a variety of social and emotional situations, experiences derived from capabilities that are common to the species, such as the abilities to feel joy, sadness and excitement, to stand erect and use the hands, to categorize, abstract and transform, to speak a language, and to learn and transmit skills.

To become a conscious, acting individual, as distinct from being a unique, reacting organism, a human being has to share and subscribe to the restrictions on communication by means of which each society maintains a universe of discourse, whose processes and patterns of thought and social interaction can be analysed as a culture (note that culture is an abstract, analytical concept: you cannot be a member of a culture). In so far as groups and individuals choose to belong or address themselves to a particular society, even the most radical innovator must sub-scribe to at least a part of its universe of discourse. The most private act of musical composition is likewise a social fact that is influenced by a set of acquired conventions. But because each individual's social experience, and consequent individuality, is unique, and because the circumstances of composition and performance are unique, it is unlikely that identical music will be created twice (except in replaying a tape or gramophone record). In this respect, novelty in composition and performance is the expected product of every musical situation and not to be wondered at.

Nevertheless, in every society there are some musicians whose compositions and performances are considered to be more original and more generally affecting than others. There is also the paradox that the more individual and personal composers are the more universal may be their appeal. One common explanation for this is that individuality and personal dominance are the most important human attributes, and the keys to cultural progress, and that in the universal struggle for survival, the less able will recognize and applaud these qualities in others and be thankful for the security that they afford. This is not the place to demolish the 'great man' theory of history (and music), except to point out that it tends to reduce communication in society to a process of domination and submission, with aggressive leaders and passive followers, so that musical performance becomes a matter of display and showing off. It also ignores the co-operative basis of tradition and invention, as well as the facts of creativity.

When people talk about creativity in terms of Muses and inspiration, they invariably refer to processes of unconscious cerebration such as Schoenberg discussed in *Style and Idea* (1951). They are, in fact, talking about ways in which the human mind works in its 'natural' state, unfettered by social and cultural conventions. They are talking about cognitive universals that all members of the species have in common. Thus one justification for the intentional use of mirror forms in music is that they are 'natural' transformations of the human mind, so that their use can hold the attention even of people who have not been trained to recognize them. Similarly, if mirror forms are innate, musicians can also use such devices spontaneously in their search for balance between variation and thematic unity. Thus musicians reared in mutually incomprehensible cultural traditions may use a common device which, because it is based on a universal mental structure, can resonate with listeners unfamiliar with the cultural or musical idiom. To do this, they must reach beyond the convention of their particular society to the universal mental processes of the species, beyond the stage of lip-service to conventional definitions of self (in terms of social status) and others (in terms of ethnic and other groupings), to an understanding of their common humanity and the reasons for variations in behaviour. This is how the most personal composers can have the most universal appeal: they communicate to others at the level of the innate; they begin with cultural conventions, but transcend them by reorganizing their sound structures in a personal, but basically universal, way, rather than slavishly following culturally given rules.

What is amazing about Mozart is not that he was biologically unique and extraordinary, as are all human beings, but that he could transcend this and become ordinary, in the sense that he was able to use powers that all people possess, to develop a skill that he had acquired incidentally through a unique set of circumstances. Thus, he has been able to share his musical vision with millions of other people, few of whom knew him personally, and most of whom have little or no idea of the social reality of his life. It is, of course, hard to prove that any of us really shares Mozart's music, rather than our own personal perceptions or re-creations of it. But there are two kinds of evidence that convince me that it is possible: first, there have been many occasions on which his chamber music has concentrated my attention and that of fellow-performers to the point where our ensemble work has been transformed, and we have felt a qualitative change and secondly, it seems that quite independently, different musicians often agree on 'magic moments' in a piece of music, even to the extent of particular bars, phrases or chords.

CULTURAL CONVENTIONS, INDIVIDUAL FREEDOM, AND MUSICAL EXPERIENCE: THE SOCIAL CONSTRUCTION OF MUSICAL RESPONSE

The communicative power of music in a society derives from the ways in which it is used to mediate between cultural convention and individual freedom, and in which an intensely personal creation can become public property. At the end of the last chapter, I gave an example from Africa to show how people have invented and transmitted a cultural convention which enables members of their society both to relate more closely to each other and to transcend the situation as individuals. The musical performance is only able to communicate to the participants because they have learned to make links between different kinds of knowledge and experience. Without those guiding patterns of human culture, they might 'quite literally, not know how to feel' (Geertz 1964:47) and be unable to relate the experiences:

In order to make up our minds we must know how to feel about things; and to know how we feel about things we need the public images of sentiment that only ritual, myth, and art can provide.

(Geertz 1975:82)

For the Venda people of Southern Africa, and for many other African peoples, musical communication in general, and the particular bodily experiences that could be generated by polyphonic performance, were linked to other experiences and ideas. Music can be profoundly moving by means of the resonance that people can establish between the tone-stress and ideal motion of music and the nervous tension and motor impulse of their bodies. But no music has power in itself. Music has no consequences for social action unless it can be related to a coherent set of ideas about self and other and bodily feelings.

There were two sets of conditions necessary for musical communication to take place and for performance to enhance the consciousness of individual Venda people:

1) A series of related but contrasting musical structures whose performance could be internally related to the content and contexts of different social situations, and
2) A coherent system of ideas that could enable individuals to make sense of personal musical experiences in terms of relationships with other people and experience of social institutions.

As I pointed out in the first chapter, music is a social fact: tonal systems, scales, rhythmic patterns, harmonies etc. are constructed and interpreted by individuals with the same cognitive equipment as other features of a socio-cultural system. An audience also 'performs', in so far as it becomes involved in the re-creation of a work (cf. Blacking 1981A:193). This point has been stressed by Clifford Geertz with the telling sentence, 'Art and the equipment to grasp it are made in the same shop' (Geertz 1976:1497). Venda music was effective when people made links between its formal structure and social content and their own experiences of life and music.

In order to understand their personal responses to music, we must understand their concept of personality. In traditional Venda society, each individual birth in theory marked the return of an ancestral spirit in human form, and the death of every 'identifiable', fulfilled person marked the birth of a new ancestral spirit. Thus every human being began life as a reincarnation of a deceased person (who maintained his/her autonomy as an ancestral spirit), and could eventually become an autonomous ancestral spirit in his/her own right. The cycle of existence was not a closed, self-perpetuating system, but cumulative as a result of the fruitful social life of individual human beings. Self could only be realised through others, but significant others only existed because of fully developed selves. Also, others could be part of self as well as witnesses of one's selfhood.

The Venda explained the apparent egoism of very small babies with the observation that they had not yet developed human characteristics. They did not yet belong to the *mu/vha* class of nouns reserved for human beings: they were *lushie* or *lutshetshe*. They would become human through association with others (*muthu ndi muthu nga vhanwe*), and their apparently selfish acts were expressions of their need to share and comunicate with others. They were, after all, ancestral spirits returning to a partly familiar world, and they wanted to reacquaint themselves with it. *Vhuthu*, the abstract noun derived from *muthu*, was used to refer to a particular person's kindness, goodwill, or charity, rather than to the general notion of 'humanity'. A well-known saying was a *hu aluwi muthu; hu aluwa mbilu*, 'it is not the person who grows up, but the heart'.

The linking of musical experience and performance to daily life began at the earliest age in Venda society,[1] when mothers carried infants on their backs while they danced and sang. Very small children joined in the choruses of the songs that accompanied story-telling at night, and they soon found that singing children's songs (*nyimbo dza vhana*) was a way of establishing personal identity and being accepted by their peers. As they grew up, some of them learnt to play certain solo instruments for personal pleasure and reflection, but all participated in the boys' and girls' play-dances (*dzhombo*) on moonlit nights, where they first learnt to improvise words and dance-steps, use additive rhythms, and lead songs – all good training for the *malende* songs and dances which were a major musical activity of adults.

If tone-stress and ideal motion in music portray nervous tension and motor impulse and so stimulate emotional experience, it is because people have learnt to make the connections. From early childhood, Venda grew accustomed to experiences of bodily change and animation that could be had through systematic body movements with others. Early training in music emphasized polyrhythm rather than isorhythm, as in the musical examples at the end of the last chapter. Sensuous, bodily experience was a consequence of correct musical performance which was to be attained by rehearsal, and correct musical performance was a way of feeling. Having feelings through music could be an end in itself or a means to an end, depending on the context of the feelings and the person having them. The collective effort, a cultural convention, produced new forms for the ears of performers and listeners. The rhythmical stirring of the body, the experience of 'falling into phase' that was necessary for the right musical sound, could be a pleasant experience in itself; or it could be interpreted as experimental evidence of the presence of the other self within the social person, and so enhance people's individual freedom and sense of personality.

Another Venda cultural convention which allowed for intense personal experience was the institution of *ngoma dza midzimu* (literally 'drums of the ancestral spirits').[2] Its effectiveness depended as much on the power of the nonverbal symbols of its music and dance as on the verbally expressed ideas and sentiments associated with it. For instance, anybody could dance *ngoma*, but only members of the cult were 'taken' by the spirits of their ancestors, and then only when they were dancing at their own homes, with which the ancestral spirits were expected to be familiar. The effectiveness of the music depended on the context in which it was both performed and heard. But ultimately it depended on a proper, rhythmically steady performance of the music by drummers, rattlers, and singers. This helped dancers to attain a somatic state in which they became more than usually conscious of the life-force in their bodies, and to come face to face with their other selves, the real self of the ancestor spirit (Blacking 1973:44–5, 1983 and 1985 *passim*).

Ngoma dances were very popular events; many people came to dance or to watch, and there was always discussion about who was possessed and how the spirits had manifested themselves. At every *ngoma*, at least four kinds of person could be moved deeply by a good musical performance, but their consequent actions were constrained by their interpretation of the 'otherness' that they felt. There were (1) members of the cult group for whom *ngoma* was being held; (2) members of the cult who came from other groups; (3) members of the audience who chose to dance or play the drums and performed well; and (4) members of the audience, such as myself, who performed occasionally or not at all. The first three kinds of people, at least, appeared to have the same intense musical experiences, but only the members of the particular cult group were possessed. People often remarked that certain lay members who danced or played exceptionally well must surely become possessed one day. This was not because good performance in itself was expected to induce or be a sign of imminent possession, but because their commitment to the dancing was thought to reflect their interest in the religious purposes of the cult or the religious life in general. It was never suggested, as it was in some other musical contexts, that a good performer of *ngoma* might be showing off. The consequence of showing off in *ngoma*, and perhaps inadvertently becoming possessed by a spirit (not necessarily of an ancestor), were too serious to have been treated lightly.

One question that arises in considering the effects of *ngoma* is, how can the same music, played on the same occasion and in the same context, affect individuals systematically in at least four different ways? Correct performance of *ngoma* gave people the chance to experience a way of feeling and relating to each other that was different from ways of feeling associated with other musical styles, and the words of *ngoma* songs emphasized that a good performance should bring out the spirits. The interdependence of parts was based on polyrhythmic principles common to all Venda music; but the tempo, the style of drumming, the length of period and of call and response, were different and *felt* different. Assuming that all four 'types' of participant were equally involved in the music of *ngoma*, why were they not all possessed? If people who had been possessed in one context were not possessed in another, can it be said their performances of the music and the dance were at fault? Such a question is irrelevant: given that a performance was adequate and some people were taken by the spirit, the crucial difference between people's responses lay in their definition of the other self who was invoked by the transcendent state of the self. In other words, two people might be moved to have a similar physiological response to the music, but only one of them would become possessed on each occasion, depending on the context of the dance.

Spectators (4) could share with *others* a common group identity, and the communion enhanced by the music was an end in itself. Good performers (3) who were not members of the cult could share a general *fellow-feeling* which transcended normal sociability, in much the same way that all music-making and dancing offered people different ways of feeling. Members of other cult groups (2) concentrated more on expressing their *selves* as fully as possible, without infringing the rights of the members of the organizing cult group (1) to exhibit their *other selves*, in the form of the ancestral spirits who returned to earthly society through their bodies.

These very personal manifestations of transcendental experience by members of possession cult groups contrasted with the state of almost corporate ecstasy that could emerge during a performance of the sacred dance *tshikona*, 'when people rushed to the scene of the dance and left their pots to boil over', when old men 'threw away their sticks and danced' and 'peace came to the countryside' (Blacking 1976:50–1). Members of possession cults could be as moved by *tshikona* as others, but on such occasions their experience of 'the other world in which things were no longer subject to time and space' were not associated particularly with their own ancestral spirits. They were associated rather with the world around them, in which 'the other self' within themselves and their fellow human beings communicated with time past and future.

FROM PERSONAL WORLD TO ALL HUMANITY?

The creation and enjoyment of music are very personal matters, although both the music and the circumstances of performance are embedded in a social and cultural matrix. A commitment to music that is almost an obsession can infect a person for life as a result of the unique ways of feeling that musical appreciation and performance can provide. But in many cases an addiction to music can take up so much of someone's personal energy that overweening egoism stifles the high-mindedness and fellow-feeling that we tend to expect from those who practise a noble art. Likewise, there are not necessarily connections between the personalities of composers and the personality of their music.

Even if one allows that certain kinds of biography exaggerate the 'demonic' characteristics of artists, there are still too many performers and composers whose lives are a sad contrast to the excellence of their music-making. I refer not to whether they boozed or womanized, which seem to me to be harmless activities, but to consistently mean and selfish behaviour or a startling lack of political consciousness.

It should be clear from what I said in the first chapter about the evolutionary value of music-making, and I hope it will become clearer in the sixth and seventh chapters, that I am convinced of the importance of music in education and in human development. How are we going to argue for the moral and educational value of music in our society, if some of its finest practitioners seem to have gained so little as human beings from the experience? There are too few musicians who have had both the ability and the generosity and nobility of Franz Liszt. This is a real problem, and it cannot be dismissed with the trite argument that the products of 'genius' justify all kinds of behaviour.

It is a problem that arises from the tasks of reconciling cultural convention and individual freedom in musical communication, and of relating art to life. It is exacerbated in feudal and capitalist societies, where there is a highly articulated division of labour and professionalization of musical life, and where the interests of individuals and their societies are culturally polarized. It was far less evident in Venda society, where ideas about self and others, and their realization in musical practice, were such that self-interest and fellow-feeling were not contradictory.

The relevance of composers' personal worlds to the rest of humanity, and the relationship of those worlds to their musical output, pose problems that were neatly encapsulated in Geoffrey Crankshaw's programme notes for the EMI Recording of the 1971 performance of Elgar's *Enigma Variations* by Sir Adrian Boult and the London Symphony Orchestra. He wrote:

In this work Elgar's alchemy lifts the particular to the plane of the universal. For his friends we may read all humanity. It is the best of aspiration and the deepest of emotions that we meet here.

These sentences are typical of much that is written about music, but they contain contradictory assumptions that cannot be taken for granted – especially if we accept that reactions to Elgar's music would be at least as varied as the socially determined responses to the Venda music of possession, *ngoma dza midzimu*.

First, I will not argue about the use of the word 'universal' because I assume that Crankshaw refers to Elgar's general outlook and attitude to the composition, and is not claiming that Elgar has written universal *music*. His world of music clearly does not have a great deal in common with Javanese, Chinese, Japanese, Indian, or Persian worlds of music.

Secondly, as I hope I made clear with the example of Venda possession music, 'Elgar's alchemy' in itself cannot do anything: its effectiveness depends on how people make sense of it. If I read 'all humanity' for Elgar's friends, it is because I know nothing about his friends, and cannot possibly feel as he did about them or about 'the places associated with his various compositions', which he pointed out to Fred Gaisberg over fifty years ago, on a drive on Saturday, 26 August 1933 (Moore 1974:212). Besides, I am not sure that thinking of all humanity rather than of Elgar's friends and their particular personalities is actually lifting Elgar's vision and music to a higher plane. My own enjoyment of the *Enigma Variations* has been greatly enhanced by my experiences of Macmillan's ballet, which emphasized the domestic and personal aspects of the music, and of Ken Russell's film, which endeared me to the sensitive individual behind the Edwardian moustache.

Thirdly, although I agree with Crankshaw that one can sense in Elgar's music 'the best of aspiration and the deepest of emotions', we cannot assume correlations between aspirations, emotions, a view of humanity, and the quality of a piece of music that is motivated by one or all of these factors. For example, some very powerful music has been written by composers whose aspirations are far from lofty. On the other hand, Alan Bush is a person whose view of humanity and practical work are admirable, but I do not find his music a compelling testimony to the power of his ideas. Similarly, when my daughter Fiona had her first complete remission from acute leukaemia, I wanted to express my feelings in a work for the choir that I conducted. On 8 March 1963 I completed an elaborate but rather indifferent piece which lacked alchemy although it was obviously inspired by 'the deepest of emotions'. In addition it got off to a bad start because I was restricted by cultural convention: although my beliefs at the time were neither orthodox nor strictly Christian, I chose to write a *Te Deum* in English. It might have been better to have written a popular song.

Geoffrey Crankshaw's remark about lifting the particular to the universal has relevance in so far as people's creativity has been shown to relate to their ability to live beyond culture and not for culture, and to have an open view of human relationships (cf. Wertheimer 1945). Creativity, as distinct from exploratory behaviour, seems to require what the psychologist Milton Rokeach (1963) called an 'open mind', and Edward de Bono later (1969) described as 'lateral thinking'. Rokeach demonstrated that the ability to think creatively and to construct new forms is a function of personality. People low in ethnocentricism reveal a comprehensive cognitive organization, while people high in ethnocentricism reveal an underlying narrow cognitive organization. Thus the most 'open mind', and hence the highest degree of creativity, belongs to those who see cultural experience in the broadest terms.

Impressive as these psychological findings are, I am none too sure that they would be found to apply consistently to creativity in nonverbal communication, and especially in music. Although I have argued elsewhere (e.g. Blacking 1973:103ff.) that there seems to be a correlation between the creativity of musicians and their positive intentions and outlook towards their fellow human beings, I have an uneasy suspicion that people whom Rokeach would define as narrow-minded and ethnocentric can sometimes produce original and effective music, and that the personality of a composer's music is not necessarily related to personality any more than it is an expression of nationality and cultural background.

My final comment on Geoffrey Crankshaw's assumptions is that a concern for all humanity is not always a deeper emotion or higher aspiration than a concern for friends. Indeed, people can be so involved with little circles of friends that they forget all about the world at large and the plight of other human beings. But so can an abstract concern for 'all humanity' block people off from the reality of actual relationships with their neighbours.

I come back to the points with which I began this section: 'the creation and enjoyment of music are very personal matters', although some cultural conventions are necessary both for developing feelings and musical skills and for communicating them to others. How composers, performers and listeners create and respond to music depends not on any single factor, such as personality, but on how they place themselves and their musical activities in relation to other activities. In some cases, personality or political consciousness may be decisive factors in the formation and effectiveness of a composer's style or particular compositions. In others, the music may be influenced by experience of a particular instrument and a concern for its sonorities and effect in performance; or, to quote Percy Grainger, the music may become

the vehicle of expression for accumulated forces, thoughts and desires, which, under less civilized conditions, more often find their normal outlet in actions.   (Balough 1982:67)

Thus the music of 'art'-composers within the same tradition, and even of the same period, can spring from as many different sources as the musics of oral traditions which I discussed in the first chapter.

Although this fact invalidates most methods of comparative analysis and requires us to look at the work of each composer with analytical tools appropriate to his/her personality and style, there are two further facts that hold out hope for some explanation of these complex phenomena, and both of them were mentioned in Percy Grainger's article in the 1915 *Musical Quarterly* which provides the title for this chapter. They were discussed under the sub-headings 'Art encroaching upon life' and 'The impress of personality: unwritten music is not standardised'.

I shall elaborate these two related ideas, and then I shall discuss the notion of ethnomusicology as social science, as a means of resolving some of these problems about the relationships between art and life, and especially personal lives.

ART AS THE BASIS OF A RICH, PERSONAL LIFE

In his discussion of art encroaching upon life, Grainger lamented that

With us moderns life is apt to encroach upon art, whereas with un-educated or primitive folk the reverse seems more often to be the case. Their lives, their speech, their manners, even their clothes all show the indelible impress of a superabundance of artistic impulses and interests. A modern Scandinavian has said of the old Norsemen: 'They were always ready to throw away their lives for a witty saying'; and much the same literary attitude towards everyday speech may be observed in the queer old illiterate cronies from whom we get the English peasant songs or sea chanties. They show little or no keenness about money or desire to 'better' themselves, but they love to be 'wags', and crowd every moment of the day with quaint and humorous sayings and antics. When finishing a song they will add: 'No harm done', or some equally abstract remark. One of the best folk-singers I ever knew, who had had the varied career of ship's cook, brick-maker and coal merchant, won a prize ('a fine silver pencil') for dancing at the age of 54, performing to the playing of his brother, who was a 'left-handed diffler', i.e., bowed with his left hand, and fingered with his right. There is a ballad called 'Bold William Taylor'[3] found all over Great Britain that tells how Sally Gray, abandoned by her faithless lover, William Taylor, dons 'man's apparel' and follows him to the wars, where she is informed that 'he's got married to an Irish lady', whereupon the two concluding verses run:

> And then she called for a brace of pistols,
> A brace of pistols at her command;
> And there she shot bold William Taylor
> With his bride at his right hand.

> And then the Captain was well pleased,
> Was well pleased what she had done;
> And then he made her a great commander
> Aboard of a ship, over all his men.

One of the best songsters I ever met, whose name happened to be Joseph Taylor (of Saxby-All-Saints, Lincolnshire) had picked up this ditty on a short absence from home when a young man. On his return he found his mother in bed with her new-born baby beside her. 'What shall we call him?' he was asked, and being just then full of the newest addition to his repertoire of 'ballets' (as they are called by the rural singers) he replied: 'Christen him Bold William Taylor', and his advice was followed. I wonder how many babies of the educated classes have been named after a song?

H. G. Wells, the novelist, who was with me during a 'folk-song hunt' in Gloucestershire, on noticing that I noted down not merely the music and dialect details of the songs, but also many characteristic scraps of banter that passed between the old agriculturalists around us, once said to me: 'You are trying to do a more difficult thing than record folk-songs; you are trying to record life'; and I remember the whimsical, almost wistful, look which accompanied the remark.

But I felt then, as I feel now, that it was the superabundance of art in these men's lives, rather than any superabundance of life in their art, that made me so anxious to preserve their old saws and note their littlest habits; for I realized that the everyday events of their lives appealed to these dirty and magnificently ignorant rustics chiefly in so far as they offered them opportunities for displaying the *abstract qualities of their inner natures* (indeed, they showed comparatively small interest in the actual material results involved), and that their placid comments upon men and things so often preferred to adopt the unpassionate formal and patterned habits of 'art' (so familiar to us in rural proverbs) rather than resemble the more passionate unordered behaviour of inartistic 'life'.

(Balough 1982:67–8)

In his section on the impress of personality, Percy Grainger emphasized the creative work of individual singers and musicians. Tape-recordings of different artists performing the same music on different occasions have confirmed that this is so of many other oral traditions. What Grainger did not make clear was that the individual renderings of competent musicians are not haphazard or lacking in conscious artistic control. That is, though one individual's version may differ from another's, performances of each version are consistent and to a certain extent standardized for that performer at a particular period of his/her life. The version has been thought out carefully, like an original composition.

Grainger commented that

The primitive musician unhesitatingly alters the traditional material he has inherited from thousands of unknown talents and geniuses before him to suit his own voice or instruments, or to make it conform to his purely personal taste for rhythm and general style. There is no written original to confront him with, no universally accepted standard to criticize him by. He is at once an executive and creative artist, for he not only remoulds old ditties, but also weaves together fresh combinations of more or less familiar phrases, which he calls 'making new songs'. His product is local and does not have to bear comparison with similar efforts imported from elsewhere.

I once let an old Lincolnshire man (a perfect artist in his way) hear in my phonograph a variant of one of the songs he had sung to me as sung by another equally splendid folk-singer, and asked him if he didn't think it fine. His answer was typical: 'I don't know about it's being fine or not; I only know it's *wrong*.' To each singer his own versions of songs are the only correct ones.

It would be difficult to exaggerate the extent to which such traditional singers embellish so-called 'simple melodies' with a regular riot of individualistic excrescences and idiosyncrasies of every kind, each detail of which, in the case of the most gifted songsters at any rate, is a precious manifestation of real artistic personality; so much so that a skilled notator will often have to repeat a phonographic record of such a performance some hundreds of times before he will have succeeded in extracting from it a representative picture on paper of its baffling, profuse characteristics.   (Balough 1982:69)

As I argued in the last chapter and as Grainger emphasized in his 1915 paper, the evidence of performances of unwritten music supports overwhelmingly the view that ordinary people are musically inventive, and that when they have a chance to be so they invest what they do with their own personal style. Art encroaches upon life because it is a primary modelling system for human thought and action. Artistic cognition is a species-specific capability which all human beings possess. Although it may be transformed into all kinds of cultural disguises, human beings have the capacity both to use it in a way that was not immediately determined by cultural tradition, and to identify it when they encounter it in the product of some other person or society – provided that they can think *beyond* the conventions of their cultural experience.

As Percy Grainger pointed out, the development of large-scale industrial societies, which require a great deal of cultural uniformity to function, has made it increasingly difficult for individuals to exercise their right to musical expression. But although musical performance has become more standardized, the impress of personality is still a crucial factor in the evaluation of composers and performers. Jazz and pop musicians, and folk-singers in particular, consciously cultivate individual styles. James Porter (1976) has described changing versions of Jeannie Robertson's performance of the ballad 'Edward' (no. 13 in the

Child collection), which she called 'My Son David': first, when she was discovered in 1953 as a traditional singer; then, when she had given some concerts to students; and thirdly, when she had become an established international folk-singer and adopted the appropriate mannerisms.

A similar study by Ruth Katz (1970) showed how the younger generation of Aleppo Jews in Israel developed 'mannerisms' in their singing of traditional music, although these were not present in performances of the older generation. They did this as part of their determination not to accept the majority group culture, and to preserve a minority tradition.

Clearly, the reasons for the impress of Jeannie Robertson's personality on her performance were not the same as the reasons of the young Aleppo Jews. And they in turn were motivated in different ways from Sir Edward Elgar. But there is no reason why these and many other different kinds of musical invention should not be compared and better understood as examples of art encroaching on life and changing it, rather than as reflections of what has already happened. In other words, I am suggesting that nonverbal behaviour, and especially music, may generate social action. Just as people learn by experience to express their feelings in culturally accepted ways, so they may also *feel* their way forward to new social and cultural formations by means of the abstract structures of music. Because large-scale musical structures have appeared in most civilizations *after* developments in architecture, it does not follow that ideas about musical form must have reflected innovations in architecture. Not only is there evidence of large-scale musical forms in unwritten music; there are also good reasons to see a progression from the invention of verses of repeated phrases in music to the idea of hoeing a field in rows or the principles of weaving, rather than vice versa.

One last thought on the innateness of artistic thought before I turn to its application in social action. There is a logical sequence from the observation of mirror forms in nature to the use of mirror forms in design, but not to their use in music. If, however, mirror transformations are a feature of innate cognitive mechanisms which make experience possible, they could be applied to any creative field without prior observation or experience.

ETHNOMUSICOLOGY AS SOCIAL SCIENCE

As Fischer has said for art, so in music 'the decisive style-forming factor' is, 'in the last instance, the social element' (Fischer 1963:152). This incorporates the impress of the personalities of individual composers, performers and listeners, as well as cultural conventions because, as I have already argued, people's ideas about personality, self, and other, and the ways in which they link these ideas to musical actions, are socially constructed. Whether the music is written or unwritten, the creation of a musical style is the result of conscious decisions about the organization of musical symbols in the context of real or imagined social interaction. Although the makers of unwritten music carry the equivalent of musical scores in their heads, their performances even of standard, ritual music can be affected by social context. For example, Venda women knew well the polyphonic *domba* initiation song; but when, after marriage, they performed it with different individuals from other villages, their ensemble work was weak until they began to know other singers personally. Similarly, performances of written music reveal subtle differences between various interpretations to such an extent that people are often less interested in the original score than in the ways in which it is remade by the performers.

Music is an ideal field for the study of relationships between patterns of social interaction and the invention and acceptance of cultural forms, which in turn may influence further action. Ethnomusicology therefore holds out great hope for resolving some problems in the social sciences, and that is why Lévi-Strauss could argue (1969:18) that music is the supreme mystery of the science of man and that it holds the key to the progress of many disciplines. The most important common problem that ethnomusicology shares with social science is how to develop a satisfactory theory of action. A social science of music must explain how compositions and musical systems are created out of individual decisions, and how in turn music-making can generate experiences that affect subsequent decision-making. Analyses of the process by which the musical content is formulated and interpreted, whether of written or unwritten music, become in essence analyses of sequences of decision-making in given social contexts, the performances by which people make new sense of available cultural knowledge.

Attention to the social element in the analysis of style does not, therefore, neglect its musical aspects, and is not concerned solely with the social background. On the contrary, what is anthropologically and sociologically most interesting about music is its special nature as a social activity and the peculiar characteristics of its symbols.

Not all social activities are analytically interchangeable. Supposing that patterns of recruitment, interaction, social class, age, sex etc. were the same for quartets of musicians, bridge-players and tennis-players, there are still important differences in the quality of interaction and experience generated by the different activities. Perhaps some activities are more likely than others to help create and maintain warm and lasting social relationships, to inspire commitment to certain ideas and actions, and even to influence social activity in other spheres. What is the effect on people of using musical symbols to initiate and regulate social interaction? Once a person has agreed to make music with others, a considerable amount of free choice in decision-making must be suspended until the end of the piece is reached. There are, of course, opportunities for free decisions within all performances, and especially those of unwritten music that encourage improvisation and personal variations from different individuals. But why are people prepared to accept situations that deny them personal freedom? What advantages do they perceive in music-making? And could they be mistaken?

The anthropologist Maurice Bloch (1974) has argued that political leaders among the Merina of Malagasy used song and dance, as restricted codes, to suppress argument and reinforce traditional authority. In contrast to this, I have claimed that in the South African context music was used to articulate a desire for political freedom that could not easily be expressed in other ways (Blacking 1981). This is not an argument about right and wrong in anthropological analysis, but a demonstration that the arts have no intrinsic value precisely because they have no obvious use. Almost every argument in favour of the moral value of the arts and the prophetic role of artists in one social context can be countered by evidence of their malicious effects and the arrogant egotism of artists in another.

One task of ethnomusicology is to find out how music might most effectively be used in human development, and whether some kinds of music are more or less susceptible to political abuse. The survival and popularity of some musics, and their apparently good effects on those associated with their performance, suggest that they have positive evolutionary value that ought to be assessed. The value of music may not be entirely at the mercy of the ways in which it is used. We need to remember that because the capacities to make and appreciate music are species-specific, and because even extreme differences of culture do not create completely unintelligible ways of feeling and thinking in people, there is always the possibility that similar methods of musical performance can generate similar responses, regardless of social context, because of their use of similar human bodies.

In the next three chapters I shall examine some of the similarities and differences in musics of the world.

3

'Irregular rhythms': movement, dance, music and ritual

THE ORIGINS OF MUSICAL IDEAS

This chapter and the two that follow are about musical ideas. They address a key question about all music, the question that stimulates many biographies of composers, histories of musical styles, analyses and evaluations of compositions and studies of performance practice: *from where do musical ideas come?*

This was an underlying theme of Leonard Bernstein's brilliant Norton lectures, *The Unanswered Question* (1976). But for many people it is a question that does not need to be answered: musicology and ethnomusicology are 'distractions' that keep people away from the important business of listening to and performing music. Rhythm, melody, harmony, and timbre are facts of musical expression, and the varieties of music and musical experience can be taken for granted as inevitable consequences of the varieties of human nature and of the creativity and preferences of individual human beings. Whether music is a system of signs that are given meanings in social contexts, or a language of emotions, or a metaphor of feeling, or whatever, *musical* ideas, as distinct from ideas about music, come from and are sustained by the musical experiences of individuals through their absorption in listening and in performance.

Rhythmic patterns, melodies, and harmony can be described as basic ingredients, and musical ideas as the omelettes, soufflés, crèmes brûlées, egg-flips and zabagliones that can be created by using different quantities, combinations and treatments of them. I can enjoy some egg dishes more than others without having to know how they were cooked, just as millions of Italians' taste for spaghetti is not influenced by the fact that the Chinese invented it. Why should it not be the same for music? Why should

51

my enjoyment be cluttered up with ideas about the sources of musical ideas? Surely, people simply grew tired of Bach's heavy contrapuntal concoctions, and wanted the lighter, frothy textures of his sons' music. When European art music was bogged down in harmony at the turn of this century, there were people who felt the need to revive it with an injection of rhythm, and so some composers dished up new mixtures of the old musical ingredients.

I have deliberately mixed my metaphors to emphasize the methodological and analytical confusion that can arise when people try to explain changing fashions in music by reference to extra-musical phenomena. But musical performance in itself will not remove that confusion or make words redundant, because the confusion is a symptom of the ambiguity that is necessary for people to make sense of musical communication. The more varied the ideas that can be related to the experience of a piece of music, the more likely it is to have wide appeal.

As I argued in the two previous chapters, rhythmic patterns, melodies, and harmony have meaning because people are able to choose to integrate different kinds of experience; they are rarely, if ever, used in different ways and in different proportions simply because of a desire for purely *musical* balance or because of some logic of musical evolution. Composers' applications of golden numbers or the Fibonacci series do not give musical forms greater and more absolute powers of communication, and the different structures of Indian *ragas* cannot ensure that the moods and concepts associated with them will be evoked by all sensitive listeners. Musical ideas are human constructs that are related to other ideas in cultural systems.

Similarly Percy Grainger's ideas about using freer, more natural rhythms and melodies in music were derived not from the facts of nature but from his *conceptualization of nature*. He frequently expressed his views about the free music of the future with words such as:

The big object of the modern composer is to bring music more and more into line with the irregularities and complexities of nature and away from the straight lines and simplicities imposed by man ... We should follow nature and allow ourselves every possible freedom of expression.

(Lloyd 1982:12)

The contradictions are interesting, and they reflect contrasts between his experiences of 'folk' music and current ideas about its status. His mixture of scientific and unscientific statements conflicts with his scientific approach to the study of unwritten music and to the composition of 'free music'. Nature is, of course, very complex, but it is by no means as free and irregular as Percy Grainger imagined. Moreover, human freedom and the development of personality have been achieved largely by the detachment from nature that is made possible by the invention of culture. And the invention of culture requires simplification and repetitions in communication. Grainger deplored repetitions in music as being redundant and undemocratic (Balough 1982: 90): they reflected the stranglehold of life upon art, while irregular rhythms reflected the freedom of nature, and the encroachment of art on life. He drew attention to the prevalence of irregular rhythms in 'folk' music, and described them as 'radical points of enrichment, inventiveness, and individualisation, evolved in accordance with personal characteristics' (Balough 1982:25).

This was a very important and original observation, because at the time it was widely held that much 'folk' music was improvised or casually strung together. No less than fifty years later, when I observed similar accuracy in performances of African music, my fieldwork supervisor expressed great surprise that this could be so. Grainger was able to make this observation because he took the trouble to record the same song by the same singer on as many as three or four different occasions:

the smallest rhythmic irregularities are repeated with no less uniformity than are regular rhythms ... This frequent uniform repetition of irregularities, goes, to my mind, to prove that very many of them are not careless or momentary deviations from a normal, regular form.
(Balough 1982:25)

In other words, Grainger recognized, as a result of thorough scientific investigation, that irregular rhythms in 'folk' music were not the result of poor performance, but the intentional expression of musical ideas. Why, then, did he believe there was something more 'natural' about them?

Grainger failed to see that musicians whose music he admired for its closeness to nature were in fact doing something that was far removed from his concept of nature. He thought that 'folk'-singers and 'folk' music were in some way closer to nature than the makers of 'art' music. In so far as they lived in rural areas, this was true; but their careful repetition of irregular rhythms was a cultural, institutionalized action that was not intended to reflect nature, and did not bring its singers any closer to nature. Grainger's conceptualization of nature was a consequence of his background and upbringing and personal friendships in Europe. As a youth in Australia, he conceived the idea of 'free music' that would reflect what he saw as the freedom of nature. Then in 1899, at the age of seventeen, he began to work out the details of the kind of music that would realize these ideals. Three years later, at the age of twenty, he had completed the first version of *Hill-Songs* nos. 1 and 2,[4] in which 'irregular rhythms' are a major feature.

Within a space of forty-four bars there are forty-two time signature changes which run after this fashion:
$5/8$, $1\frac{1}{2}/4$, $2\frac{1}{2}/4$, $3/4$, $4/4$, $2/4$, $1\frac{1}{2}/4$, $5/16$, $3/4$, $5/8$, $1\frac{1}{2}/4$, $2/4$, $7/8$, $5/8$, $4/4$, and so on.
(Bird 1982:60)

Hill-Song no. 2 was scored for twenty-four solo winds and cymbal and described as 'Large room music'. I find it a poignantly beautiful piece, and I could not 'get it out of my system' for weeks after first hearing it. It epitomizes for me the character of the young, acutely sensitive Grainger. It is important to remember that Grainger wrote this music *before* he heard and studied 'folk' song. It was not until four years later that he recorded and noted the repetition of irregular rhythms in 'folk' song. This seemed to provide for him a justification of what he had done and was planning to do as a composer.

By 1907, at a time when Stravinsky was working on his Symphony in E flat, Grainger had sketched a piece called *Sea Song* wherein rhythm had become almost indeterminable, not to say unperformable. The first thirteen bars – bearing, incidentally, the instruction 'Fast' – provide the following time signature changes:
$1/4$, $7/32$, $3/32$, $5/64$, $5/16$, $3/8$, $7/64$, $3/32$, $5/64$, $9/32$, $3/8$, $7/64$, $5/16$.
(Bird 1982:60; see also Lloyd 1982A:115)

Grainger stated that his 'studies in the rhythms of prose speech …in 1899 led to irregular barrings' (Balough 1982:85). The irregular rhythms in much 'folk'-singing come from the same source as Grainger's artifice, though the ultimate aim is different.

The irregular rhythms of John Maguire's version of *Molly Bawn Lowry*,[5] for instance, are the result of *undoing* the metre of the verses into which the words were originally organized, and so making them less like other Irish music, which is characterised by the regular rhythms of jigs, reels and hornpipes. He did that not because he wanted to revert to nature or to prose, but because he was concerned to 'tell a story' as effectively as possible (Morton 1973:154–5).

I have frequently encountered systems of unwritten music where, as in Ireland, master musicians tend to go against the general trend of their musical tradition – though that tendency was itself a tradition.

Thus, the distinguished Ugandan harpists Temusewo Mukasa[6] and Evaristo Muyinda were admired because of their facility with words, whose irregular rhythms contrasted strongly with the instrumental ostinato. Bob Marley's famous song *Rat Race*[7] was almost entirely declaimed rather than sung. In Venda, song (*-imba*) was distinguished sharply from speech (*-amba*) by the organization of words into a metrical framework,[8] and the aim of musical development in the chorus section of songs was to create a rich counterpoint of sound that removed the song as far as possible from the structure of the words that inspired it.[9] But the music of semi-professional musicians (*zwilombe*) was expected to be rich in words and topical commentary.[10]

A musical idea such as that of irregular rhythms can therefore come from a number of sources. Percy Grainger justly claimed that his own use of the device sprang from the conscious develop-ment of sounds that he first heard in his mind, and that Cyril Scott used the same technique in his Piano Sonata Op. 66 of 1908 with his 'enthusiastic permission'. What is not so certain is the direct link with Stravinsky's *Rite of Spring* of 1913, which Grainger implied in an article that he wrote in 1949 (Balough 1982:85). Moreover, Grainger's own use of irregular rhythms in later years was influenced by his experiences of 'folk' song and by other, extra-musical ideas that he brought into the formu-lation of his musical ideas.

Musical ideas can therefore emerge from the purely musical imagination of individuals, or as reflections and transformations of other ideas. Clifford Geertz has insisted that 'an artist works with signs which have a place in semiotic systems extending far

beyond the craft he practices' (Geertz 1976:1488). He quoted
from Michael Baxandall's *Painting and Experience in Fifteenth
Century Italy* (1972) and emphasized that different domains of
Renaissance culture contributed to the way fifteenth-century
Italians looked at paintings: 'Piero della Francesca tends to a
gauged sort of painting, and Botticelli to a danced sort of painting'
(Baxandall 1972:152), and those tendencies catered for the
interests of different social groups. Geertz's argument implicitly
accepts an important principle of anthropological analysis, the
notion of patterns of culture, or the coherence of cultural
systems, by which sets of ideas and institutions within a community are structurally interrelated.

A gallant attempt to apply this principle worldwide to the
analysis of music and dance systems has been made by Alan
Lomax (1968, 1972), who has argued that the different technological systems represented by the cultures of the world correlate
well with their systems of music and dance. There are a number
of problems with this global scheme: for example, Lomax com-
pares only the surface structures of the music without asking
whether the same musical sounds are always produced by the
same process. He also seems to assume that a correlation means
that the music reflects the ethos or eidos of a culture: it could
in fact be *counteracting* social trends.

Lomax's scheme does not explain from where musical ideas
come: it only suggests how they are related to other ideas in a
cultural system. He takes the categories of rhythm, melody and
harmony for granted, rather than treats them as problematic. Of
course, we can never know exactly how the basic musical ideas
were invented; but at least we can look for the origins of particular ideas in different social and cultural contexts. Although
irregular and regular rhythms are both cultural phenomena, we
must not neglect the possibility that in some situations a musical
idea could be a product of pure imagination, a reification of
abstract thought, and not merely a reflection or transformation
of some other idea. We must keep in mind the possibility that
human beings possess an innate capacity for musical thought,
or at least for a kind of cognition which is most characteristically
realised in musical forms.

An important writer who turned his mind to this problem just
before Grainger began thinking about irregular rhythms and

discovered 'folk' music was Karl Bücher. One of the most remarkable things about Bücher was that he had the courage to change his mind and refute an earlier theory when he came across evidence that contested it. His earlier theory is well known; his modification of it is less well known but much more significant as a guide to understanding the origins of ideas about rhythm. In 1896 he published his book *Arbeit und Rhythmus*, in which he produced musical examples from all over the world to elaborate his theory that music had its origin in production, in the rhythms of work.

Bücher provided numerous examples to show that in all societies each time of the year had its particular 'work-sounds' (*Arbeitsgeräusch*) and each type of work its own music (Bücher 1896:36); that rhythms had an influence on work (*ibid.*:27–30), but that the techniques of work also shaped work-songs (*ibid.*: 42–3, 51–2, 359 etc.). He contrasted the songs that accompanied the joyous, carefree, occasional work of spinning, with those that accompanied the serious, heavy, daily work of grinding (*ibid.*:83, also 73 and 78 ff.). He quoted the example of a Maori *Totowaka*, in which rhythms and music were heavy or light, slow or fast, according to the difficulty of the ground over which a canoe was being pulled, or the weight of loads carried (*ibid.*:172–5).

In East, Central and Southern Africa, I heard many work songs and frequently noted the kinds of relationships between form and use which Bücher identified. Whenever women pounded maize together, the speed of their song increased and the sound of the pestles became sharper, as the maize was gradually transformed into flour and the stamping block was emptied. (This can be heard for example, in my recordings of Nsenga music, Ethnic Folkways Library FE4201, side one, bands 4–6.) When Venda women pounded and winnowed at the same time, two often pounded in duple time, whilst a third shook the winnowing tray in triple time. I could not determine to what extent these performances of typically Venda (and African) cross-rhythms were deliberate productions of basic musical figures, or the chance results of the concurrence of two different work-rhythms. Women considered it smart to tap rhythmically the sides of the winnowing tray with their thumbs, in order to complement the pounding, and they would also sing in time to the pounding, whether or not they 'made music' with the tray. But on other occasions they might work together without attempting to synchronize the rhythms. Thus the same people performed the same operations in different ways, sometimes 'musically' and sometimes 'non-musically'.

Work songs, therefore, were not determined so much as constrained by the rhythms of work. For example, women pounded in the same way in different parts of Zambia, but not all pounding songs were like the Nsenga melodies cited above: length of period and patterns of melody and tonality of Gwembe Tonga songs were systematically different, as Tonga and Nsenga musical styles differed. Moreover, many songs sung at work were in fact adaptations of songs designed for other social activities.

These facts support the kinds of argument which led Karl Bücher to modify his hypothesis. In the original edition of *Arbeit und Rhythmus*, he had proposed, wrongly, that 'primitive' people appreciated only rhythm, but not tone and harmony (Bücher 1909:42 and 381). He went even further: in the ninth chapter on *Der Rhythmus als ökonomisches Entwicklungs prinzip*, he asserted, as part of his general economic theory of history, that *all* music was derived from the rhythms of work, and that the economic principle had been manifested from the earliest moments of human history through rhythm, which enabled people to labour with the minimum of strain and waste of energy. As part of his general argument, Bücher emphasized that the sharp distinction between work and play was a relatively recent development in the history of mankind (*ibid.*:5 and 16); and it was in this area of his thinking that his study of Karl Groos's books on play in animals (1896) and human beings (1898) seems to have influenced the reversal of his original theory.

In his book *Industrial Evolution* (1901), Bücher suggested that the existence of an economic principle presupposes a 'pre-economic stage of development, that is not yet economy':

How economic activity was evolved from the individual search for food can today hardly be imagined...Labour among primitive peoples is something very ill-defined. The further we follow it back, the more closely it approaches in form and substance to *play*.

In all probability there are instincts similar to those that are found among the more intelligent of the lower animals, that impel man to extend his activities beyond the mere search for food, especially the instinct for imitating and for experimenting...

All regularly sustained activity finally takes on a rhythmic form and becomes fused with music and song in an indivisible whole.

It is accordingly in play that technical skill is developed, and it turns to the useful only very gradually. The order of progression hitherto accepted must therefore be just reversed: play is older than work, art older than production for use.   (Bücher 1901:27–8)

PLAY, RITUALIZATION, MOVEMENT AND MUSICAL IDEAS

The idea that the evolution of an 'artistic' process was the crucial development in the emergence of the human species is not new. It was, for instance, suggested 250 years ago by Vico, who argued that human beings danced before they walked. The biologist, Professor J. Z. Young, has said that the capacity to create new aesthetic forms has been the most fundamentally productive of all forms of human activity. If we consider the earliest Acheulean artefacts of the Stone Age, made some half a million years ago, their most striking feature is not their function, as instruments of production, *but their form*. Functionally, as tools, there was no need for them to be shaped as they are. They are not more efficient. What is important is that some of the earliest evidence of organized production of tools is also evidence of an 'artistic' or 'aesthetic' sense, of a new way of thinking and of new ways of feeling and moving the body. To quote Professor Young:

Whoever creates new artistic conventions has found methods of interchange between people about matters that were incommunicable before. The capacity to do this has been the basis of the whole of human history.
(Young 1971:519)

In *How Musical is Man?* (1973), and in several works on Venda music, I tried to show how musical forms are modelled on social life and various features of cultural systems, and I quoted Le Roi Jones:

Music can be seen to be the result of certain attitudes, certain specific ways of thinking about the world, and only ultimately about the 'ways' in which music can be made.   (Jones 1963:153)

I do not dispute that. But I want to consider an alternative approach to art and life which was advocated by Percy Grainger and which might be paraphrased thus:

Human attitudes and specifically human ways of thinking about the
world are the results of dance and song

– not necessarily dance and song as we know them, but a form
of adaptive behaviour that was the prototype of dance and song
and, I believe, most other forms of specifically human behaviour.

Exercise of the artistic process, of which dance and song are
the most elementary products because they are contained within
the body, is a special kind of exercise of sensory, communicative
and co-operative powers that is as fundamental to the making and
remaking of human nature as speech. Dance and song can be
understood as primary adaptations to environment; with them,
mankind can feel towards a new order of things and feel across
boundaries, while with speech, decisions are made about boundaries. This is why even in industrialized societies, the changing
forms of music may express the true nature of the predicament
of people before they have begun to express it in words and
political action. In South Africa, Black consciousness was expressed in music many years before it emerged as a serious focus
of political activity.

Although our understanding of the musics of the world is not
yet sufficient to provide any conclusions about musical cognition
and the genesis of musical ideas, I find it useful to keep in mind
a general picture of the way in which music can relate to other
kinds of collective experience.

In the first chapter, I discussed music in the context of
biological evolution and asserted that music-making, as a technique of the body, could mediate between culture and nature,
invention and evolution, continuity and change. Musical performances are both transmissions of a cultural tradition and
adaptive responses to unique social situations. In the second
chapter I discussed some problems of musical communication,
with special reference to the communication of personal vision
by means of cultural convention. I now want to extend some of
the arguments and place musical activity in the broader context
of collective behaviour.

Firstly, human beings are by nature social, educable, and
highly sensitive as a result of their encephalated nervous system.
In the processes of adaptation and natural selection, the unit is
not the individual but the *population-in-environment*. The

sharing of ideas and feelings is so fundamental to the process of becoming human that the species would be better called human-and-fellow-human being. We are not born human, but only with the potential to become human through social interaction with others. We are not born with the ability to speak, but only with the potential. And if we cannot exercise that potential with others at the right age, we may never be able to speak.

As Charles Darwin pointed out, the environment of human beings, as social animals, is *not* 'competitive, savage, and brutal', but co-operative; and therefore the fittest human beings are ultimately the most co-operative and those who exercise to the full the extraordinary sensory capacities of the species. I will not press the point, but in my view most of the behaviour that is described as paranormal, such as clairvoyance and telepathy, is normal. If it is rare in our modern industrial societies, it is because these capabilities have been suppressed by unfavourable cultural conditioning.

Secondly, although it is hard to believe it in the contemporary world, humans are not only social but subject to the force of *phylic communion*, the sense of being members of the same species. The importance of phylic communion and the heightened perception of the world that it provides are major subjects of music and the arts, and powerful factors in daily decision-making. The most famous expression of this sense of species brotherhood is in the Meditation of John Donne's Seventeenth Devotion:

No man is an island, entire of itself; every man is a piece of the continent, a part of the main. If a clod be washed away by the sea, Europe is the less, as well as if a promontory were, as well as if a manor of thy friend's or of thine own were: any man's death diminishes me, because I am involved in mankind, and therefore never send to know for whom the bell tolls – it tolls for thee.

One of the distinctive characteristics of many animals is ritualization behaviour, which is a manifestation of phylic communion and in several species of birds is associated with maturation and mating. In human beings, similar behaviours are situational rather than maturational, in that they can occur whenever members of the species come together – as in a celebration of Mass, a Quaker meeting, an orchestral concert, a football match, a pop festival or a family meal. Another common experience of phylic communion is falling in love, which can occur at any stage of life and to people of different societies brought up in different environments. It can be the most startling manifestation of phylic communion, because it can be quite abstract, in that those who fall in love may have no common language or cultural ties to bond them.

Those who are familiar with Emile Durkheim's (1912) analysis of Australian aboriginal ritual and totemism may recognize that I am referring to similar situations. Durkheim argued that conceptual thought was derived from a process that may be called 'religious', and he believed that it was not necessary to place humanity's distinctive attributes beyond social experience. Concepts of time and space, for example, arose from awareness of the intervals marked by communal festivals and by people's experiences of coming together for ritual and then dispersing in cycles of greater and lesser intensity of social interaction. He was refuting Kant's statement that although 'all our knowledge begins with experience...it does not follow that it all arises out of experience'. Durkheim's argument for the social determination of thought cannot be sustained because, as Stephen Lukes has pointed out, 'the operations of the mind and the laws of logic are not determined by, or given in, experience, even in social experience' (Lukes 1973:447). Lévi-Strauss has further refuted Durkheim's claims on the grounds that the most elementary social life 'presupposes an intellectual activity in man of which the formal properties...cannot be a reflection of the concrete organization of the society' (Lévi-Strauss 1964:140). In other words, Durkheim's critics have made the same kind of claim as Karl Bücher and Percy Grainger, although Durkheim himself was also arguing for the primacy of dance and music in the form of religious ritual.

Now it is true that Durkheim's phrase 'communal festivals', as we are accustomed to think of it, presupposes that social beings were thinking conceptually and probably using speech in order to create some kind of social and religious organization. But can we not envisage 'communal festivals' as times of intense social interaction in which movement and music, and perhaps other 'artistic' activities such as body-painting, were the only forms of communication? Is it not possible to have worship without words and dogma?

The performance of ritual by *specific* social groups presupposes the existence both of concepts and of groups in conscious association, as Lévi-Strauss rightly argued. But Durkheim's theory includes the possibility that ritual behaviour could generate both categories of thought and conceptualized social groups; it allows for a distinction between a *generalized communion* of people and *particular communities* of people. The intellectual conditions for the operations of the mind and the laws of logic could exist in the body, but they would not be revealed until a special kind of social interaction transformed a generalized communion of people into a particular community of human beings. The formal properties of human intellectual activity are therefore brought out by rhythms of social interaction. I prefer to call the first kind of association *'generalized sensori-motor communion'*, in which nonverbal communication predominates.

Underlying my discussion is the assumption that human behaviour is an extension of capabilities that are already in the human body, and that the forms and content of these extensions are generated by interaction between bodies in the context of different environments.

Human thought is profoundly affected by experiences of others. Thinking conceptually is not simply isolating and grouping together the common characteristics of a certain number of objects; it is relating the variable to the permanent and seeing patterns in life that transcend individual sensations. If we can understand how private sensations are transformed into concepts, which by definition must be shared and sharable, we may know how evolutionary animal instincts become the conscious human strategies that are the basis of cultural 'evolution'. Durkheim argued that private sensations can be transformed into concepts, and a more permanent pattern in life can be perceived, when people contrast their experience of periods of intense and sporadic social interaction.

I suggest that periods of intense social interaction are most deeply experienced and most likely to generate conceptual thought when inner feelings are publicly shared through a counterpoint of body movement. I am simply proposing the corollary of what many teachers of dance or gymnastics reiterate: if 'the movement is in your thinking', I suggest also that ideas may come from movement. And just as an important aim of dancing is to be able to move *without* thinking, to *be* danced, so I suggest that we strive to be moved to think, to *be* thought. It is sometimes called inspiration, insight, genius, creativity, and so on. But essentially it is a form of unconscious cerebration that is most evident in artistic creation: it is a movement of the body. We are moved to creative and reflective thinking as a result of greater intensity of feeling.

Studies of patterns of co-operation, play and gestural communication in primates and the 'dances' and 'songs' of birds and other animals, suggest all kinds of antecedents for ritual in human beings. But human beings are unique in that they combine so many of these forms of behaviour that are found independently amongst different species, and organize their social interaction into cycles of corporate and sporadic movement, greater or lesser social intensity, 'sacred and profane', and so on. Sooner or later, all discussions of human origins come up against the crucial issue of a qualitative difference between human and non-human primates. Whatever this difference is, it must exist in the human body and it must have been present at the time when a distinctly human species began to evolve. The most quintessentially human behaviour should be that in which humans are both most like other animals and least like animals. In other words, it is behaviour that allows them to be either closest to the animals as organisms reacting to the forces of nature, or furthest from the animals by the exercise of a will that can transcend nature. The organized movement of human bodies, a generalized kind of ritual behaviour, is the only human activity that can be said to extend from unconscious bodily resonance with the environment to a conscious rejection of the world of nature in the stillness of prayer or meditation, or simply non-movement.

One can speculate on the origins of such ritual behaviour in grooming practices; in increased contact between mothers and children; in pair-bonding and protracted, face-to-face confrontations in sexual intercourse; or in play. I am concerned here only with the possible effects on the body, and particularly the brain, of a kind of behaviour that would have been easy to learn and pleasurable to the individuals concerned, and would have become a fundamental adaptive mechanism because of its benefits for social life (cf. Washburn 1968:22). Available skeletal evidence suggests that the Australopithecine gait was more a run than a walk, and that the hand and the foot became human before the brain. The regularity and rhythmic requirements of communal 'dancing' would have assisted changes in motor behaviour from sporadic, short runs to a steady, walking stride. It is even possible that the rings of stones at Bed I at Olduvai and some Acheulean sites could have been the remains of dancing grounds: in Africa, I have seen rings of stones both where an area has been cleared for dancing and where stones have been brought and left as a sign of the numbers of people attending a ritual.

The kind of ritual behaviour that I believe is peculiar to the human species is more than an extension of the work routines of insects, the formal interaction of nonhuman primates, the displays of birds, or the mating dances that bond some animal pairs. It is basically a form of communion whose adaptive function is to generate greater sensory awareness and social co-operation: the sharper experience of individual consciousness that is felt in the context of collective ritual reinforces the co-operative conditions required for the experience.

Because we do not know how animals feel, we cannot say whether the content of human experiences of ritual interaction is qualitatively greater than the experiences of other animals, except in so far that the complex human brain and encephalated nervous system are likely to be more receptive to environmental stimuli and so to create greater sensory tensions in the body. But we can say that there is an important difference in *the forms of* adaptive ritual behaviour in humans and other animals. In animals adaptive ritual behaviour is specialized and matu-rational, whereas in humans it is generalized and situational. That is, the species-specific, and hence adaptive, ritual behaviour of humans, as distinct from the ritual actions of *some* humans, must co-ordinate in time all who happen to be within an im-mediately observable and/or ultimately conceivable space (thus including the physical absence of other known people, alive or dead). Experiences in time and space are therefore externalized in an *externally* given situation, so that theoretically any number of members of the human species can interact ritually at any time of life. For most animal rituals, the choice of time and place seems to depend on *internal* factors such as the stages of matu-ration of those involved.

There is, of course, much human ritual that, like animal

ritual, is restricted to certain members of the species at certain times of life, and it may be adaptive in the context of different cultures. But, as Van Gennep and others have observed (e.g. Van Gennep 1960:65ff.) the time of performance of a ritual may transcend the time of the maturational event that it celebrates (see also Blacking 1969B:4–5), and distinctions between rites that all members of a society undergo at some time or another and those that affect only some members, are generally functions of social divisions within the society.

We have come full circle back to Percy Grainger's argument that irregular rhythms are natural. Having argued at some length that both irregular rhythms and Grainger's conceptualization of nature are cultural, I have now developed the idea that some irregular rhythms could be natural in origin, in so far as they express *human* nature.

First, it can be argued that many cultural forms are natural in origin. They are the realization of discoveries about the body and its relations with its environment which have been made with the capacities of the body and are therefore extensions of it. The archetypal situation for such discoveries is the corporate move-ment of social interaction, or ritualization behaviour; and the consequence for individual bodies is personal ecstasy or what Abraham Maslow (1964) called 'peak experience'. In such con-ditions, because of phylic communion, people can become exceptionally aware of inner self, self, others and natural environ-ment. It follows that if in a state of ecstasy my body *is moved*, the patterns of movement can be structured in a number of ways. They can express mental structures, the mechanics of my limbs and muscles, and even stages in my phylogenesis. That is, if I move like a reptile, it is not necessarily because I am consciously imitating a reptile: it is because my body carries the memory of my reptilian ancestry. My movements can express elements of the self that I have acquired through experience in society, such as tendencies to aggression, submission, domination, sensuality, or even a period of military training. My movements can comp-lement the feelings and movements of others who are present with me, or they can relate to the rhythms and sensations of the natural environment. It is clear to me, from reading Percy Grainger's biography, that he was frequently in a state of ecstasy. His running from the piano to the end of the concert hall and back was a typical explosion of ecstatic movement, and his frequent jumpings up and down were characteristic movements of an ecstatic person which have been enshrined culturally in ritual dances and forms of worship.

The kinds of movement to which I refer may be called proto-dance. They are often accompanied by sounds, which I shall call proto-music. I may clap or slap my body, beat my feet on the ground or produce other kinds of noise by encountering some object in the course of a foot or hand movement. My breathing may change and the muscles of my throat may move to produce all kinds of vocalizations. My diaphragm may feel constricted until I burst into impulsive shouting or singing. When I am with other people in the same state, the possibilities of formal expressions of inner states are obviously multiplied.

I have described the sorts of movement and sound that can emerge from the body in a state of ecstasy or altered consciousness. I am suggesting that dance and music are cultural developments of proto-dance and proto-music, and that one important purpose of these arts is to restore, if only temporarily, the open state of cosmic consciousness that is the source of their existence. The process of communication is like that of a telephone or tape-recorder, in which sounds are converted into a magnetic code, which can then be translated back into the original sounds.

In general, then, we can say that dance and music are forms of ritual communication whose utilitarian value is to enhance co-operation and educate the emotions and senses. The basic capabilities are innate, in that each individual body carries the necessary equipment; but no individual body can produce more than proto-dance or proto-music without sharing experiences with other bodies. The basic model for dance and music is *human* nature. Dance and music have been discovered rather than invented. Indeed, the task of choreographers and composers is to invent cultural forms that faithfully represent the force and vision of their discoveries.

In the first chapter, I described how the performance of an elementary polyrhythm can help people to attain a heightened state of consciousness. In this chapter, I have been suggesting that different polyrhythms could have been brought out 'into the open' and into human consciousness through patterns of interaction that were generated by states of corporate ecstasy, or ritualized behaviour, similar to those that polyrhythmic playing is meant to produce. Thus irregular rhythms, or any other musical idea, can spring from different sources. They can be discoveries or inventions. They can be the expression of discoveries about the structures of the brain, discoveries about structures of social interaction, or discoveries about patterns of human personality and of the natural environment, as Percy Grainger suggested. Or they can be inventions that are puzzled out and concocted with and from other ingredients of a cultural system.

The irregular metre of the song called 'Gege of seven strokes' was intended to portray the falseness and tricky character of the deity Yemoja *in the context* of the pantheon of the Sango cult of Recife and the associated music (Segato 1984:476–7). In other contexts the same metre might not be seen as irregular or awkward.

The complex barring of Stravinsky's *Rite of Spring* and the irregular rhythms of songs of the Venda girls' initiation school, *vhusha*,[11] are typical of music that poses an old analytical dilemma. To what extent does their excitement and emotional appeal arise from the deliberate, culturally embedded creation of musical tension (cf. Meyer 1956)? And to what extent is it derived from the resonance and relaxed 'harmony' that can be achieved by a union of human artifice with natural design? Stravinsky's rhythms can quite easily be rearranged (and more easily conducted!) by regrouping the patterns and ignoring the bars.

Ex. 4a Regrouping of rehearsal nos. 186–201 of Stravinsky's *Rite of Spring*, according to rhythmic patterns characteristic of traditional sub-Saharan African music. This is an alternative way of making sense of the music which ignores the composer's barring.

Ex. 4b   Diagram of rhythmic patterns of songs of the Venda girls' initiation
schools *vhusha* and *tshikanda*, showing their interrelationships (derived from
Fig. 1 in Blacking 1970:8).

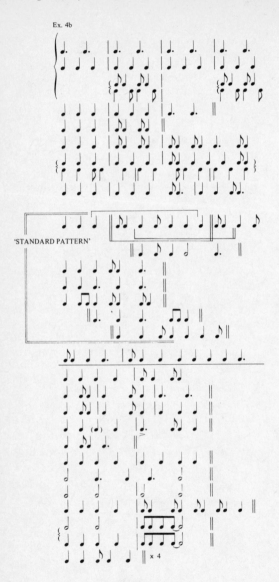

4

'The world's most lovely melodies': form and feeling in unwritten music

FORM AND EXPRESSION

In 1934, Percy Grainger wrote that the world's most lovely melodies were to be found in folk-songs. Because folk-songs were mostly without accompaniment, he argued, composers could concentrate their creative powers upon expression in a single line, without having to worry about 'harmony, musical form, the tone colour and blends of various instruments, dramatic considerations, and the like'. Grainger believed that free melodic movement allowed for rich emotional expression, and he imagined a music of the future

consisting of free and unpredetermined melodic lines of sound – swooping through tonal space in gradual curves as a bird sails through the air, untrammelled by those arbitrary divisions of tone called scales. In such free music all tone might be in a state of endless flux and it is easy to imagine such music being capable of more soulful expressiveness than any past or existing music. (Appendix A:160)

Some unwritten melodies seem to fit that specification, but they are not necessarily intended to be more expressive than music which does not, simply because they use certain glissando techniques. Many of the folk melodies that Grainger admired, such as the Londonderry Air, were in fact based on clearly defined scales or modes. Ethnomusicological research has shown that melodic invention is frequently influenced by modal systems, such as the Arabic *Maqam* or Persian *Dastgah*, in much the same way as it is influenced in European art music by harmony or musical form. In Venda music performed between 1956 and 1966 there were few, if any, pure melodies, and modality, tonality, speech-tone and harmony exerted different degrees of influence. Several scholars in the 1920s and 1930s argued that the melodies of music outside the Western harmonic tradition must be analysed as 'pure melodies', unrelated to a harmonic framework or to scales, in the sense of a fixed store of notes on which melodies are based. This view of unwritten music can no longer be sustained (cf. Blacking 1967: 176). For instance, not only were Venda melodies carefully patterned, but their patterns were organized within modal frameworks.

Ex. 5   The opening of a Venda children's song, with repeated patterns modified by a chosen mode. The diagram shows how it would sound if it were a 'pure melody' with repeated patterns but no mode.

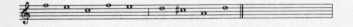

Writing about folk melodies at the same time as Grainger, Constant Lambert commented on their lack of developmental potential with the statement

To put it vulgarly, the whole trouble with a folksong is that once you have played it through there is nothing much you can do except play it over again and play it rather louder.   (Lambert 1966:146)

In Grainger's contrast between folk melodies and the themes of art music, and in Lambert's disparaging remarks about what he called 'the country pub school of composers' and their use of folk melodies, one senses a conviction that form and feeling are antithetical. Grainger seems to have been saying that form restricts the expression of feeling, while Lambert sees form as the essence of the musical art.

When I was at school, I found it very difficult to cope with this same confusion about form and feeling. My composition teacher complained that melodies which I had felt, lacked form and that those that I constructed carefully were arid and unlovely. When he demanded accuracy in my piano performance and my grand-mother complained that I practised without feeling, I felt that both my technical skill and my integrity as a person were under attack. I was not able to relate correct performance to the right feelings, as did Venda musicians, because 'feeling' was some elusive, Teutonic quality that one added to music when one got the notes right. In Venda, however, when the rhythm of an alto drum in *domba* was not quite right, the player was told to move in such a way that her beat was part of a total body movement. She could then play with feeling precisely because she was helped to experience the physical feeling of moving with her instrument and in harmony with the other drummers and dancers. There was no suggestion that she might be an insensitive or inadequate person (cf. Blacking 1973:110).

In this chapter, I hope to reconcile apparently conflicting ideas about form and feeling, which I consider to be a consequence of the pathological mind/body dichotomy that is part of the ideology of some cultures, chiefly as a result of the division of mental and manual labour in production. Music is not *either* a system of signs that are given meanings in social contexts, *or* a language of emotions, a formalized expression of feelings that are organized in order to have wider and greater effects on human action. It is both of these. Form without feeling is sterile, and feeling without form is unlikely to be socially effective.

Instead of joining battle and supporting one or the other view, we ought to ask why such arguments should ever have arisen, and whether they reveal anything useful about music itself, as distinct from the attitudes to music of different individuals and social groups. For example, the treatment of music as a system of signs, as form in tonal motion, is justified on the grounds that the range of human feelings has been much the same throughout human history and round the world, and therefore it is the *variety of musical forms* which distinguishes music from other activities and constitutes a major human achievement.

Interpretations of musical ideas range between extremes of absolutism and relativism, from viewing music as an action autonomous to treating it as an epiphenomenon of social life. What is rarely explained in anything but subjective or vague terms is why, from an absolutist standpoint, some musical ideas should be judged better, lovelier, or more complex than others; or how, from a relativist standpoint, musical ideas in themselves reflect or convey meaning about social life, unless they are quite specifically imitative – as are the cuckoos in Beethoven's 'Pastoral' Symphony and Delius's *On First Hearing the Cuckoo in Spring*, or the collages of familiar sounds in Charles Ives's music. The contradictions of formal analyses and assessments are revealed when writers and critics have to include feeling and extrinsic content in their discussions, when they claim that a brilliant technical display has no emotional content, or that a beautiful feeling has been sloppily expressed in sound. Musicians cannot ignore such inconsistent judgements, because words influence the reception of audiences, and consequently the sale of tickets. Besides, the demands of listeners, who expect to be excited by virtuosity and moved by intensity of expression, have influenced the development of musical ideas as much as the creativity of composers.

Technical virtuosity and depth of expression are not incompatible or contradictory if they are conceived as complementary processes, and if we remember that there is what Susanne Langer called 'a life of feeling' (Langer 1953:372), which is influenced by the public images of culture (cf. p. 35 above). It is important to treat feeling as a rational function, as Robert Witkin points out in his important book, *The Intelligence of Feeling* (1976), and to recognize that 'emotion is essentially a purposive, creative state' which 'raises, transforms and symbolises' (Hillman 1970:130– 1), as Carl Jung has argued. It is not helpful to draw distinctions between the emotional and the cognitive. Above all, the feelings which people express or receive through the medium of music are drawn from a repertoire of collective sentiments as much as from personal experience.

EMOTION, FEELINGS AND THE FORMS OF MOVEMENT

In chapter 3 I made a case for what we might call 'the ecstatic origins of elementary musical ideas'. I argued that the essential ideas for dance and song are results of discoveries about the body and its relations with its environment which have been made by exercising bodily capacities in special types of social interaction. I called these situations 'generalized sensori-motor communion', and compared them with ritualization behaviour in other species of animals. They are archetypes of the specific, culturally coded, sacred associations of particular communities, the communal festivals which Durkheim discussed in his analysis of Australian aboriginal totemism.

Observation of the cultural *forms* of such states shows transformations of individual facial expression and body move-ment, and of the corporate movements in space and time of the bodies involved. 'Waves' of feeling are generated in the body and between bodies, not unlike fits of sneezing or hiccoughs, and discrete sequences of tempo and patterns of movement can be discerned, analogous to the ebb and flow of a piece of music. Obviously, the forms that the movements take are much affected by their cultural framework; but at the same time a general pattern of interaction and movement can emerge, which, though often related to cultural experience, is shaped from within the body and monitored by patterns of energy flow that transcend people's conscious attempts to manipulate the situation.

I gave examples of work-songs that were not derived from work situations, and of irregular rhythms that were articulations of much larger, corporate movements of bodies in space and time. I wanted to show that although both irregular and regular rhythms are cultural phenomena as are all musical systems, some rhythmic ideas are natural in origin in so far as they express in movement aspects of the structures of human bodies. In many musical systems, and especially in Africa, irregular rhythms are perceived as whole patterns, or 'gestalts', and not as uneven subdivisions of a regular metre or accretions of different metres, as Percy Grainger and Cyril Scott conceived them. That is why I produced an alternative phrasing of rehearsal nos. 186–201 of Stravinsky's *Rite of Spring*, which dispensed with the frequently changing time signatures and portrayed larger waves of movement. One of the musical functions of irregular rhythms in African music is to intensify its timeless quality and drive forward its cyclic structures. This also makes possible polyphonic solutions to the problem of expressing continuous movement, which I shall discuss in the next chapter. In this chapter, however, I want to consider how melodic ideas might be derived from archetypal experiences of continuous movement.

Manfred Clynes, who is a neurophysiologist and concert pianist, has claimed that there is a biological basis for sharing emotion through music. This tallies with the work of another neurophysiologist, Karl Pribram, who had demonstrated that emotions are neural processes that structure input as an alternative to instrumental action, and so influence patterns of thought and imagination. Clynes has proposed a theory of 'sentics', by which he means the scientific study of the communication of emotion (Clynes 1977). He discovered that it was

possible to measure the expression of fantasized emotions, because people expressed them in very similar and predictable ways. The important factor to characterize...was the dynamic quality of the expression rather than the particular part of the body used...this quality could be isolated in the emotional expressions of an arm, a leg or a tone of voice.   (Clynes 1974:51)

Clynes argued that there are biologically determined, expressive movements that are programmed into us, and he calls these 'essential forms'.

When we feel anger, we tend to express it in definite 'angry' ways and not in other ways...Emotional gestures...have precise representations in the brain.   (Clynes 1974:51–2)

Clynes also distinguishes between an *acton* and an *idiolog*:

An acton is a particular type of action: a single, programmed, expressive action (with a duration of approximately 0.5 to 3.0 seconds) which has a clear beginning and end; the term also includes the decision giving rise to the action...

An idiolog is a single, natural thought of a quality such as sweet, red, or anger, together with certain electrical and chemical correlates in the brain. Idiologs are thus distinguished from a person's peceptual experience of a quality. Specific qualities produce definite brain responses, as experiments with colors and shapes, as well as emotions, have shown.
(Clynes 1974:52)

The point that interests me is Clynes's claim that musicians produce essentic forms all the time in their compositions and performances: they 'can generate an emotional state by repeatedly producing its typical expression'. He demonstrated this by tests such as a detailed examination of Toscanini's performances of the Brahms 'Haydn' Variations with the NBC symphony orchestra in 1935, 1938, and 1948, and by asking musicians to think musical works, as if they were singing or performing them, and at the same time to 'conduct' with one finger, maintaining continuous finger contact with a pressure transducer. Toscanini's times for the Variations changed very little over the course of thirteen years, and Clynes attributed this to a constant conception of the music and great precision of emotion. The tests of finger pressure showed that different musicians sensed in different works of the same composer the same characteristic inner pulse, as well as different inner pulses for different composers.

Clynes referred to the work of the musicologist Gustav Becking, who in 1928 had observed that one could not 'simply transpose a phrase from Mozart to Beethoven − even if the phrase is almost identical note for note − without stumbling over the phrase while conducting', because 'the underlying musical pulses are quite different' (Clynes 1974:55). 'Without the inner pulse, the individual phrases of Mozart cannot sound "Mozartian"' (Clynes 1974:54). Other composers also produced characteristic pulse shapes, and Clynes believes that the same should apply to any well-defined musical style. 'Both in composing and interpreting', he concluded,

There is a continuous interplay between the dictates of the inner pulse and the expression of particular essentic forms. Every composer... invokes most of the spectrum of emotions, but the point of view from which the emotions spring [i.e. the particular, individual inner pulse] influences their realization in sound.   (Clynes 1974:55)

I have dwelt at length on Manfred Clynes's work, because it throws more light on some problems of musical communication which I discussed in the second chapter; it emphasizes the fundamental role of body movement in generating musical ideas, and relates to what I said about form and feeling in African music; and it has implications for music education and the development of people's musical capacities. For example, Clynes writes,

Technical ability in music *should* refer to the ability to reproduce the precision of essentic form, and not merely to reproduce the letter of the written music. Precision devoted to the letter only is a wasted effort, a waste of years practicing by many students and performers.
                                                (Clynes 1974:53)

Although I am not altogether convinced by the data, methods and arguments presented in Clynes's book, *Sentics: the Touch of Emotions* (1977), they provide a particularly fresh and challenging starting point for cross-cultural studies of the relationship between musical ideas and feelings. Clynes's approach does not conflict with the ethnomusicological standpoint that I emphasized in earlier chapters, because he is concerned with measuring the expression of '*fantasized* emotions', which are of course cultural products, and his essentic forms for the specific emotions of anger, grief, hate etc. need not be universally associated with those emotions.

Even so, the cognitive aspects of musical ideas, and even of emotions, are somewhat neglected in Clynes's arguments. I prefer to think even of basic emotions as socially constructed personal behaviour, rather than as part of the human biogrammar. By this, I do not mean that emotions are entirely learned, although Watson and the behaviourists made an impressive case for this by showing that babies don't exhibit certain emotions until they have had many months' experience of interaction with others (Bridges 1932, Strongman 1978:181-2). Nor do I mean that emotions are products of the different lives of feeling that have been created as parts of cultural systems, as Clifford Geertz has suggested; that expressions of jealousy in Venda, in England, in Ireland, and in Bali, are so unique that jealousy cannot really be described as a universal emotion. I mean, rather, that *emotions are structured, inner movements of the body that acquire and are given meaning in the contexts of real or imagined social situations.* Like music, emotions are forms of bodily motion that are assigned meanings and so become expressions of feelings.

THE SOCIAL CONSTRUCTION OF FORM AND FEELING WITH THE INTEGRATED MIND

In chapter 3, I discussed phylic communion and the general conditions of co-operation and sharing that are species-specific and necessary for becoming human, and I emphasized that in the process of adaptation and natural selection, the unit is not the individual organism but the population-in-environment. Apart from this general condition of bonding with other members of the species and some sharing of somatic states, human beings inherit only motor and cognitive capacities, and possibly certain modelling systems such as verbal language, which can be used singly or in combination for communication, but whose expression and meaning are *neutral*. That is, a vigorous, rapid movement of one human being towards another is not inherently violent or angry; it could equally be loving and peaceful. Its meaning depends on what message it is intended to convey. People are not by nature aggressive or non-aggressive, and violence or peaceful living are not aspects of human behaviour which can be isolated: they are parts of complexes of behaviours that must be treated together. Emotions and feelings, like musical ideas and cultural forms in general, are the results of intentions to mean something. They are products of the power of mind, which evolves out of people's application of innate motor and cognitive capacities in social situations.

Human cognitive and motor capacities are linked not only by the fact that important milestones in motor development, such as sitting, crawling, standing and walking, are related to children's cognitive development, but also by their systematic differentiation in the left and right hemispheres of the brain. The limbs of the left half of the body are linked to the right hemisphere of the brain, and the right limbs to the left hemisphere. Similarly, the left and right visual fields, which are phylogenetically an extension of the sense of touch, are projected onto the right and left visual cortices.

Research into the lateralization of brain function has shown that

the left hemisphere is predominantly involved with analytic thinking, especially language and logic. This hemisphere seems to process inform-ation sequentially ... The right hemisphere, by contrast, appears to be primarily responsible for our orientation in space, artistic talents, body awareness, and recognition of faces. It processes information more diffusely than the left hemisphere does, and integrates material in a simultaneous, rather than linear, fashion.   (Ornstein 1973:87)

The specialisation of the two hemispheres seems to be unique to human beings and to be related to the evolution of language ... The comple-mentary workings of our two thought processes permit our highest achievements, but most occupations value one mode over the other ... *a complete human consciousness should include both modes of thought*.
(Ornstein 1973:92)

The heightened states of consciousness to which I referred in chapter 3, the states in which we are moved, we are danced, we are sung, are states in which both cerebral hemispheres are working complementarily. (This has been shown by, for example, research into the brain activity of people practising transcendental meditation.) Capacities for what I referred to generally as 'artistic cognition', and in particular for dance and music, are associated with the right hemisphere and with non-verbal modes of communication, which are considered particu-larly appropriate for expression of the quality and intensity of feeling (Bateson 1973:388). This does not mean that all artistic activities are exclusively products of right hemisphere activity: for example, many professional musicians use the left hemis-phere for music-making. Thus the location of dance and music, or speech, or emotional expression, or any other activity, seems to depend *not on the nature of the activity but on how it is pro-cessed*. We should therefore be looking not for species-specific abilities for music, as I argued in *How Musical is Man?*, but for species-specific modes of thought that can be used in processing, structuring, and communicating sensory data, and perhaps for one or two that are most characteristically realized in 'music' – which is, of course, a convenient gloss word that covers a multitude of conceptualizations of music.

I am not suggesting that musical ideas should or could be reduced to applications of these two contrasting modes of thought

to human sensori-motor capacities, or that we can now abandon
the search for subsets of a larger domain of knowing, for more
specific mental structures and schemata. We should be asking
the same sorts of questions about music that Lévi-Strauss asked
about myth and kinship. If such a mode as 'musical thought'
exists, need it be connected specifically with the organization of
tones, rhythm, or timbre? Could it be a more general mode of
thought whose most effective and characteristic embodiment is
with musical symbols? If so, in what other forms can 'musical
thought' appear? Is architecture, for example, an embodiment of
'musical thought'? Are mathematics or any of the sciences
organized with 'musical thought'?

I will return to this problem later. I have discussed the contrasting modes of consciousness of the left and right hemispheres
of the brain, their integration, and the social construction of
emotion, feeling, *and* musical ideas out of experiences of form
in motion. I have done this because the ideas of melody and
polyphony, which are the subjects of this and the next chapter,
can be seen as alternative cognitive solutions to the problem of
maintaining *in sound* the continuity of motor movement which
is generated by the kinds of ecstatic experience that I described
in chapter 3. Continuity of movement, and hence of the experiences associated with it, can be maintained simply by continuing
to move. But this cannot be done with purely vocal sound, for
the simple reason that people run out of breath.

There are two alternative ways of getting round this particular
problem. One is external, communal, and incorporates others,
by the use of polyphony, which will be discussed in the next
chapter. The other is internal, individual, and stretches the body,
by means of the invention and extension of the idea of melody.
An illusion of continuity can be created by the repetition of
phrases and groups of phrases, and by alternating shifts of tonality
which are comparable to the repetition of dance movements to
the right and then to the left, or vice versa. Real continuity can
be created by tricks of breathing; by the invention of wind
instruments and the use of circular breathing, as in playing the
didjeridu; or by the invention of instruments on which indefinite
continuity of melody can be maintained, as in bowed strings.

The problem of composing extended melody, particularly
without repetitions, absorbed Percy Grainger. He had set out to

achieve this in *Hill-Songs nos. 1 and 2*, and in 1933 he wrote a curious article in an American magazine, *Music News* (September/October), entitled 'Melody versus Rhythm'. Bartók was encouraged to reply, and in the same magazine in January 1934 he refuted 'Grainger's basic idea and suggested that rhythm and melody never were nor ought to be in conflict and that both had their parts to play in ancient, primitive and modern music' (Bird 1976:206).

Whether or not Grainger saw Bartók's reply, he was quite unrepentant in the fourth of his broadcast lectures of 1934:

I take it for granted that it is the office of the highest flights of music to uplift us, to emotionalize us and to awaken and increase within us the wellsprings of dreaminess, livingness and compassionateness – in other words, to prepare our natures for some kind of angelic life (presumably here on earth) and to turn our thoughts away from the worldly and 'practical' things of life.

It seems evident to me that it is melody and harmony rather than rhythm that are empowered to turn our natures towards the angelic state. What do we mean by melody?...Melody, I take it, is single-line sound that follows the nature of the human voice, [which] in the main...favours long, continuous sustained legato sounds – 'Prolonged utterances'.   (Appendix A:164–5)

Grainger's attack on rhythm was directed not so much at rhythm per se, which as I have already argued in chapters 2 and 3 can both help people to achieve the angelic state that Grainger reserved for melody and be a product of that state. He was chiefly concerned with abuses of rhythm:

Rhythm is a great energiser, a great slave-driver; and the lower types of mankind (the tyrants, the greedy ones, the business-minded people) have not been slow to sense the practical advantages to be drawn from rhythmically-regular music as an energising, action-promoting force. When these 'hard-headed' practical people want young men to go and get themselves killed, they play marches to them; and they encourage sailors and roadworkers to sing at their jobs in order that the maximum of hard work may be forthcoming as economically as possible. The practical-minded people welcome any type of music that will encourage themselves and others to dance rather than to dream, to act rather than to think.   (Appendix A:165)

There was, however, one type of rhythm which Percy Grainger found uplifting. After a final salvo in which he stated that 'the slave-driving, soul-stultifying influence of rhythm lies in regularity and repetitiousness and in all the four-bar phrases and other forms of musical platitudinousness and inventive torpor that these give rise to', he concluded:

On the other hand, subtle, irregular, unrepetitious rhythms hold fine influences towards freedom and rapture,   (Appendix A:166)

as in Cyril Scott's *Solemn Dance* for six strings, piano, harmonium and bells and Claude Le Jeune's (b. 1528) *Pretty Swallow* for six voices. He described these works as 'examples of melodious irregular rhythm', and he could have added many further examples from the music of sub-Saharan Africa, where musicians are primarily concerned with the *melodies* that ensembles of drummers produce.

THE PROBLEM OF THE SONG TEXT

Grainger's broadcast lecture of 1934 on 'Melody versus Rhythm' began with a quotation from the Chinese *Record of Rites*, said to date from 2255 BC, which highlights another problem in the creation of melody — the conflict between music and words, which have formed the inspiration for so many melodies:

Poetry is the expression of earnest thought, and singing is the prolonged utterance of that expression.

The problem of words and music is a problem of melodic composition as old as the sung word, and it occupied Richard Strauss and Clemens Krauss in the opera *Capriccio*, which they called 'a conversation piece for music in one act'.

FLAMAND	So then we are –
OLIVIER	Loving enemies –
FLAMAND	Friendly opponents –
OLIVIER	Words or music –
FLAMAND	She will decide it!
OLIVIER	First the words – then the music!
FLAMAND	First the music – then the words!
OLIVIER	Music and word
FLAMAND	Are brother and sister
OLIVIER	A bold comparison!

Combining words and music is not just a matter of uniting text and melody in an agreeable harmony. It is a basic problem of human expression which has far-reaching implications: can the music and the speech modes be combined with equal attention to both without subordinating one to the other? Will words detract attention from music? Or vice versa? And if so, why? Will the physical strength and cultural priority of the brother dominate, or the moral force and natural superiority of the sister? Will either words or music dominate under all circumstances, or only under special conditions?

The expressive powers of words and music were compared in Strauss's *Capriccio*. But the argument was slightly confused, because two types of verbal discourse were referred to interchangeably and without distinction. For example, the composer Flamand sings, 'Music is the root, the primary source. The sounds of nature sing at the cradle of all arts... The cry of pain preceded language'; the poet Olivier replies with the philosophical truism, 'But only speech can explain pain.' Then he goes on to say; 'The real depth of the tragic can only be expressed in poetry.' To equate poetry with speech is to blur a crucial distinction between words and music. Speech can be propositional as music cannot be: you can argue with words in ways that you cannot argue with music. But poetry is more often like music – 'redundant, illocutionary and performative'. In some musical systems, there is no distinction between poetry and music: in Venda traditional music, for example, rhythmically recited verse was classed as 'song'.

For the sake of argument and progress in theory, it is useful to draw clear boundaries between speech and song; and so I will not discuss poetry. On the other hand, it is equally important *not* to draw boundaries between cognition and affect, as Olivier and Flamand tend to do, nor to characterize speech as cognitive and music as affective and to make Eurocentric psychological assumptions in analysing relationships between speech and song, words and music.

It is often assumed that song is an extension or embellishment of speech, which is the primary mode of communication, and that there is a continuum of increasing formalization from speech to song. But song is not inherently either a more or a less restricted code than speech: the relative dominance of song or speech, as of their affective and cognitive elements, in any genre or performance of a genre, depends not so much on some absolute attributes that speech and song might have, as on people's 'intentions to mean' in different social situations, and on their motivation and the psychological assumptions that they invoke. In order to understand how song and speech are generated and interrelated as products of the human body, we must first investigate different folk uses, perceptions and conceptions of words and music, speech and song, and the sets of psychological assumptions about human nature and society in which they are embedded.

In Venda, during the 1950s and 1960s, people denied that there was a continuum between speech and song. They recognized formal links, but they made a sharp distinction between what they regarded as different modes of discourse. *Within* the realm of music, however, there were distinctions between melody that was free and melody that was word-dominated, melody that was influenced by the speech-tone patterns of words and melody that could follow the logic of musical discourse. Similarly, in the *ukom* drum-row music of the Igbo of Nigeria, Joshua Uzoigwe (1981) has shown that composers derived their melodic patterns from two contrasting sources, which were glossed as 'drum-text' and 'drum-sound'.

Again, in Irish traditional music, there is a distinction between songs that 'tell a story', in which the story is the most important element, and songs with words that express emotion *about* a situation or a story, but are not meant to tell a story. Further, *dance*-tunes are given names but carry no text.

One can find examples of a gradual transition from speech to song; but again this does not prove that it is based on a 'natural' tendency to shift from one to the other. The kinds of cases that I have encountered are culture-specific and depend on context: a shift from the speech of a sermon to a hymn in a South African Independent Church could be explained by the fact that the sermon itself was presented in a musical, call-response form and the aim of the whole event was spiritual expression.

There is not much ethnographic support for the notion of a continuum between speech and song, and so it is useful to turn once more to the lateralization of brain function. It seems as if speech and music may be produced with the help of two different, though relatable, systems and that they cannot easily be united on equal terms. They can be combined in song, but complementarity is not the same as unity (e.g. you could not *unite* the attention required to drive a car in heavy traffic and to carry on a complicated discussion without almost certain disaster, but you could combine them with unequal attention to each task). Moreover, if we take Strauss's analogy, we should certainly not commit incest and unite brother and sister!

What was the solution of the heroine in *Capriccio*? She did not have the option of polyandry, and so she could not marry both Flamand the musician and Olivier the poet. Nor did she select one rather than the other, because she loved them both for what they were. And so she refused them both, and chose the pleasure of the situation in which they were united only in their unfulfilled love for her. Richard Strauss, as philosopher of the arts, took the view that words and music could be united in song, and especially in opera. But Strauss, as musician and composer, seemed to take a more personal view, and, if we follow the brother/sister metaphor, one appropriate for a patriarchal society. At the end of the opera, the music (the brother) dominates in a flourish of melody that makes the words redundant (rehearsal nos. 270ff., especially 282–4).

The important point about Strauss's argument, as about the ethnographic evidence, is that neither words nor music are supreme, and they can never really be united on equal terms. The choice does not depend on psychic forces but on the decisions of individual human beings.

The analysis of human intentions becomes the key factor in understanding the relationships between music and speech and their significance in human experience. *Music and speech have no intrinsic power to dominate as cognitive systems, because of some proved or unproved hierarchy: emphasis on one or the other, or any attempts to unite them, are the consequence of their uses by human beings in social contexts.*

The only possibility of reconciling music and speech rests in the ability of human beings to respond to the total sound impressions without regard to either the music or the speech meanings. This requires that listeners create for themselves *new* meanings in response to the noises that reach their ears. Inevitably, these interpretations may differ from meanings that would be derived from the words or melody on their own.

Songs can provide test-cases for discovering more about musical thought, if such a thing exists, because people's perceptions of and responses to tensions between words and music, text and melody, can indicate how they use and value contrasting but complementary modes of discourse. Problems to resolve are, for example, how words suggest ideas that generate melody; how musical ideas find more precise forms through words; how words generate melody, which develops a force of its own and in turn generates new words. The forces can be musical and the forms verbal, or vice versa. The notion of 'musical' thought suggests that there are musical forces which are more general and less culture-specific than, say, a dominant resolving to the tonic, a pathogenic melody descending from high to low pitch, or a rhythm increasing in speed and intensity.

If there is such a thing as musical thought, it will be discovered not through applying some analytical rule-of-thumb to a variety of musical compositions and musical systems, but by describing the coherence of different musical systems and the structures of their musical ideas in terms that reflect as accurately as possible the concepts, intentions and perceptions of those who use them. If common factors emerge from such diversity, we may one day be able to talk of musical processes that are as universal as the elementary structures of kinship and verbal languages.

The first step in the analytical journey is to concentrate on cases where the tension between song and text is properly exemplified. A song or its text may be taken out of the context in which it was originally composed, and given a new meaning for an occasion which need have no connection with its form or content. This is particularly common with songs used for political purposes, such as verses set to a National Anthem or to hymns. The texts may be very interesting, but they are not *song* texts properly speaking. Such situations may reveal much about the uses of melodies or the uses of words, but not about the dynamic tension of speech and music modes used together.

To identify the elementary structures of musical ideas it will be necessary to peel away all features that can be explained in terms that are not specific to music. In song, in particular, it is necessary to discover how speech and music interact and how one mode affects the other.

For example, in the Venda musical system, there were several different kinds of relationship between words and melody, and in order to understand the relative influence of each mode on particular occasions, it was necessary to find out what people thought they were doing.

(1) Words in a song did not have to tell a story. A string of words could be slotted in as appropriate for a particular occasion or type of song. They were *'presented'* as a finished artefact without requiring thought about the details of their content. They had symbolic meaning in the context of a song, without necessarily specifying or referring to what they could mean in ordinary verbal discourse.

(2) There was not necessarily any connection between the mood or sense of words and the structure of melody. Even the same song could be described in one context as a song of joy and in another as a song of sorrow (see Blacking 1973: 43).

(3) Words influenced the structure of melodies in a purely formal sense, because of the control which patterns of speech-tone had over the formation of the opening phrases of songs and of parts of each subsequent verse (Blacking 1967:*passim*; Blacking 1973:69–70).

(4) Music could shape the composition of words, especially in improvised passages. The musical framework of a song, established by the opening phrase, influenced the structure of additional verses that were invented, and sometimes connections of meaning could be musical rather than verbal. Thus one verse might be composed to succeed another not because it pursued a verbally expressed idea but because its words repeated a pattern of speech-tone that had been portrayed in the melody of the previous verse.

(5) Words were abandoned altogether as a song progressed, so as to allow for further *musical* development, with freer movement of parts in counterpoint (Blacking 1973:70–1).

(6) The whole structure of a song could be influenced by structures characteristic of musical rather than verbal thought. For example:

1. *Ihi, nwana wa nwananga!*
   Ihi, nwana wa nwananga,
       Vhasa mulilo!

Ihi, Vhasa mulilo?
Ihi, Vhasa mulilo,
    Baba vha a vhuya.

Ihi, Baba vha a vhuya.
Ihi, Baba vha a vhuya;
    Vha vhuya na nnyi? etc.   (Blacking 1967:120–3, 134–6)

2. *Thathatha' Thanga dzi a swa,*
    Nde' Dzi a swa:

Dzi a swa na Vho-Maramba
Na Vho-Nyundo.

Vho-Nyundo vhe' Ri ya 'fhi?
    Ri ya shondoni; etc.   (Blacking 1967:118–20, 132–3)

There is also a feature of speech communication that relates it both to song and to the body movements that give rise to song. David Abercrombie argued that

all rhythm . . . is ultimately rhythm of bodily movement . . . our perception of speech . . . depends to a considerable extent on the hearer identifying himself with the speaker. As we listen to the sounds of speech, we perceive them not simply as sounds, but as clues to movements. It is an intuitive reaction of the hearer to be aware of the movements of the various organs which the speaker is making. We perceive speech in muscular terms.

Speech rhythm . . . is *in* the speaker, and it is in the hearer in so far as he identifies himself with the speaker. We might coin the term 'phonetic empathy' for the process . . .

The rhythm of speech is primarily muscular rhythm, a rhythm of bodily movement, rather than a rhythm of sound.

(Abercrombie 1965:19)

This relates to my argument in the previous chapter about play, ritualization, movement and musical ideas (p. 59ff.), and to the notion of music as a sonic extension of bodily vibration. It leads on to the next chapter, in which I discuss the implications of Percy Grainger's idea that there are links between polyphonic sound production and the experience and practice of democratic social order.

5

'Democratic polyphony': political and musical freedom

'DEMOCRATIC SCALES', HETEROPHONY AND POLYPHONY

In the first chapter, I challenged the notions that musical ideas evolved from 'simple' to 'complex', from one-tone to five-tone, seven-tone, and twelve-tone scales, and that the complexity of these ideas was related to the technological complexity of cultures. Ethnomusicological research has shown that the history of music is not related to the acoustical properties of sound, except when people choose to link it to the harmonic series, as did Paul Hindemith and the ancient Chinese. It has also shown that polyphony is not a logical or inevitable development of any particular modal system, and that the invention of scales and their use in polyphony have followed a variety of patterns.

In Venda, for example, five-, six-, and seven-tone modes are used, but they do not represent stages in musical evolution. Much of the music of the aboriginal clans was based on a seven-tone scale. A five-tone scale was introduced by invading clans about 200 years ago. Sometime during the early nineteenth century, the Venda's neighbours to the South, the Pedi, borrowed from them the idea of reed-flute ensembles, but they adapted them to their own pentatonic scale. Subsequently, the Venda borrowed back from the Pedi their pentatonic reed-flute music. *Tshikona* is therefore older than *matangwa*. Both scales were considered suitable for a hocket-like type of polyphony, in which each player blew only one tone on a stopped pipe[12] (Blacking 1971:*passim*).

Tshikona was for the Venda sacred music (*ngoma*), while *matangwa* and its modern variants were play music (*mitambo*). I shall be discussing this important cultural category in the next chapter on work and leisure.

   The Chinese settled for a five-tone scale, although they were
well aware of and had used other, more 'complex' scales. They
preferred it because of the clarity of its larger intervals and the
significance of the number five in Chinese cosmology. Their
acoustical system was derived from a cycle of overblown fifths,
whose tones were produced by blowing across a set of bamboo
tubes which were arranged in mathematical proportion. The
twelve pitches (*lü*) had specific names, and they were arranged
into pan-pipes and chimes in two groups of six tones each,
representing the complementary forces of *yin* and *yang*. The first
five tones of the twelve *lü* became the basic scale of Chinese
music, and the sixth and seventh were used as passing tones. The
Aymara of the Andean highlands are one of many other societies
who use pan-pipes and male–female classifications (Grebe-
Vicuna 1980, Chacón 1981), but although Chinese musical
theory and practice are very ancient, there is not evidence of
diffusion from China.
   Sophisticated musical systems are not the prerogative of
civilizations, and there is no more reason why the music of the
Andean peasants should have been derived from ancient Inca
music than the *ganga* of Bosnia and Herzegovina should have
been a degeneration of urban music (cf. Petrovic 1977:*passim*,
and p. 15 above). We do not have to look further than Australian
aboriginal cosmology and kinship systems to know that complexity and a potential for great sophistication of thought are
characteristics of the human mind. Claude Lévi-Strauss emphasized that a technologically simple society

is not a backward or retarded people; indeed it may possess, in one realm
or another, a genius for invention or action that leaves the achievements
of civilized peoples far behind.   (Lévi-Strauss 1963:102)

   One of the most important developments in European tonal
music, which allowed for the kinds of formal expansion beyond
what Constant Lambert saw as the restrictions of 'folk' song, was
the adoption of equal temperament. It could be described as a
democratic development, in that it abolished the acoustical
hierarchy of keys and made possible the standardization of pitch
and freer exchange of musicians, and ultimately the rejection
of tonality in favour of the twelve-tone row of equally valued
tones. This might be described as the ultimate in 'democratic

polyphony', but unfortunately many of those who have used this as a basis of composition have not been democratic either in their political outlook or in their attitudes to music, music-making, and fellow musicians.

There is little doubt that in principle the equal spacing and weighting of tones allows for polyphonic expansion, since it enables several parts to move freely and independently at the same time. In practice, however, equal-stepped scales seem to have been invented mostly in societies with hierarchical political structures and a corps of professional musicians who were able to maintain the musical instruments and keep them tuned. The most common technique in some Asian societies, where equal-stepped scales were used long before equal temperament was invented in Europe, was heterophony. This is neither polyphony nor democratic. David Reck describes it as

the weaving of melodic strands around a central core of melody; it is melody-based (rather than harmony-based) and its strands, happening simultaneously, all relate to the central melody in some way.

(Reck 1977:312)

Curt Sachs described heterophony as being like a group of very different people massed together, as in crossing the street, and walking in the same direction. It is a sort of polyphony, but clearly not a 'democratic polyphony'.

Javanese and Balinese music have been classified as heterophonic, but it is now more common to describe their systems as 'colotomic', which is a term referring to a sort of polyrhythmic heterophony. As in heterophony proper, all instruments follow a basic melody which is repeated like a passacaglia or ground bass, but they play variations in relation to different, but concurrent, rhythmic cycles.

There has been considerable scholarly debate about whether or not Javanese scales were equal-stepped, and whether or not their xylophones and scale-systems had been diffused to Africa. In Buganda, where there was a hierarchical political structure under the Kabaka, with semi-professional musicians who were called into the palace to provide music for the King, musicians seemed to be concerned to produce an equal-stepped five-tone scale on their xylophones, bowharps, lyres, and tuned drums (see Wachsmann 1950). Lois Anderson (1968) has described how

Ganda xylophone melodies can be transposed into different modes (*miko*). Although in theory an equipentatonic scale is required for this, in practice it seems that the scale is not exactly equal-stepped. Nor is the method of playing heterophonic: it is polyphonic.[13]

Gilbert Rouget has published a record of music played on seven-tone xylophones by Mandinka from Guinea,[14] who are heirs to one of the former West African empires. The keys of the three xylophones are tuned with great accuracy to a scale that divides the octave into seven equal intervals (Rouget 1969). They are not played in the same way as the Ganda xylophones, since the players do not share the one instrument.

Hugh Tracey claimed that the xylophones of the Chopi of Mozambique, in South-East Africa, were also equiheptatonic. Their orchestras were first described by a Portuguese missionary in the sixteenth century, and judging by his description, it seems that the basically heterophonic style of performance has not changed greatly, though new melodies and new orchestral suites have regularly been composed[15] (Tracey 1948).

What is interesting about the Chopi orchestras is that the political system in which they thrive does not appear to have been hierarchical, as were the systems in Buganda, Java, and some other Asian countries, and the musicians were neither court musicians nor belonged to a separate professional class. They were villagers, who also played xylophones, rather like the Balinese. I emphasize this point in order to make it clear that I am *not* proposing some kind of equation between equal-stepped scales, heterophony, and hierarchical political systems. The same or similar musical ideas can be associated with a variety of social systems, and vice versa.

The polyphonic singing of the San hunter-gatherers of the Kalahari and of the Babinga of the Ituri forest took people by surprise, because such societies should not have been performing the kind of music whose invention was supposed to have been a European achievement (see p. 10 above). And yet it is surprising that people should have been surprised; because polyphony is probably the most natural of all musical ideas. Colwyn Trevarthen (1979) and others who have researched mother–infant interaction, have shown that canon and counterpoint and polyphony are the earliest forms of interaction in human development, especially during the period when infants begin to express more specific emotions than a state of excitement. They have not used those particular musical terms, but the words are most appropriate to describe the harmony of head and eye movements, and the patterns of touching and cooing and gurgling that can be observed.

San and Babinga polyphony tends to be made up of short melodic phrases that are bound together by a hocket-like means of production similar to that used in Venda reed-pipe dances (Blacking 1973:51). There is no competitive tension, as there is in the Inuit throat games[16] (Beaudry 1978, 1980; Nattiez 1983), where the interaction is 'agonistic' rather than 'hedonistic'. Thus, three different societies of hunter-gatherers, from tropical forests and tropical and arctic deserts, have invented distinctively different musical systems.

However natural and democratic infant–mother counterpoint may be, San and Babinga polyphony are no less cultural than the techniques that were introduced into European art music when composers incorporated the musical styles and mensuration of dances. The vocal monody of plainchant was intended to express 'the Catholic ideal of a spiritual world unity' within the framework of a church dedicated to God (Mellers 1950:56 and *passim*); its style contrasted with the regular rhythms of secular dancing and the 'tonic–dominant' relationships that occur in lively pieces such as *Sumer is icumen in*. Is it surprising that the early masters of polyphony came from the Netherlands and England, where the peasants had become free during the thirteenth and fourteenth centuries respectively?

Although the advent of polyphony in Europe signified a move towards the sort of political freedom that is expressed in the polyphonic music of the San and Babinga, it carried with it certain restrictions which, as I pointed out in the last chapter, Percy Grainger thought inimical to human freedom. Any attempt to bring together several voices or instruments requires some agreement on pitch, tonality, modes, and especially metre, unless the music is to be aleatory. The expressive freedom of melody can be restricted in the interests of polyphonic texture and participation, and similarly some modes and scales may be less suitable than others for polyphonic treatment.

Percy Grainger's argument needs to be taken seriously, because it raises the spectre of the arts being used to dull the political consciousness of the masses with vicarious entertainment, like the bread and circuses of the Roman emperors, and to support the hegemony of certain classes.

MUSIC AND POLITICAL FREEDOM

There are many ways in which music can be used in the cause of political freedom, as well as to advertise the power of kings. In traditional African societies, political commentary was often expected from minstrels, who were immune from any reprisals provided that they *sang* their protest. Unfortunately, this tradition has not been maintained: Ugandan musicians were murdered under the tyranny of General Amin, and in Nigeria the pop-star, Fela Kuti, was imprisoned.

The political content of Venda music was not always directly expressed in words. Polyphony was an important element of political expression because its performance involved the support of many people. Different styles of music within the Venda musical system as a whole signified the identity of different social groups, and so musical sound could express the size of their membership, and be used to settle a dispute. In 1956, a chief took a company of supporters to install his candidate in place of a district head whom he no longer favoured. He stopped at the foot of the hill where the head lived and his supporters played *tshikona*, which, amongst other things, was the statutory music for the installation of a ruler. Supporters of the district head heard the music and quickly gathered to play a rival *tshikona* on top of the hill. Before long, it was clear to all from the volume of the music of the two *zwikona* that the chief did not have as much support as the head, and so he returned home without pressing the case of his candidate further.

On another occasion, some years before I arrived in Venda, a famous Chief, Ratshimphi, was fed up with the actions of the white Native Commissioner, and so he gathered a force of over 350 *tshikona* players and went to Sibasa 'to honour the Native Commissioner' before making 'a small request'. The sound of the musicians dancing round the District Offices brought all court and clerical work to a halt, but the Chief pointed out that to stop the music would be seen by his supporters as a loss of face for the Commissioner. As a result, the Chief's request was granted and the Native Commissioner was reminded noisily of the sort of support that Ratshimphi could command.

I appreciate that such cases belong to a kind of village politics that one associates more with a tradition of French film comedies than with the harsh facts of modern nation-building and urban confrontations. However, modern African political songs played an important role not only in transmitting verbal messages in pleasant ways that were easily recalled, but also in binding together in a common cause people who came from different ethnic groups and spoke different languages. This was achieved by the *sounds* of the music, which symbolized a modern way of life with cities, industrial technology and schooling. In 1959, when I was transcribing Venda music on a farm in Kwa-Zulu, unschooled Zulu peasants responded positively to the sounds of Venda 'school' songs even though they had no idea what the words meant, whereas they had shown absolutely no interest in the sounds of Venda traditional music. In other words, they were divided by their traditional musics, but united by the sounds of modern music, which had blended African modality and polyphony with the tonic–dominant chordal procedures of European hymns and part songs (Blacking 1980).

In some African states where nationhood was assured, it was not uncommon for political songs to use modernized versions of traditional genres. In 1965, in Lira, in the north of Uganda, the local MP had a supporting group who composed and sang political songs, accompanied by an orchestra of mbiras of different sizes. The result was as musically beautiful as it seems to have been politically effective.

POLITICS AND MUSICAL FREEDOM

Most of the examples that I have given can be described as political uses of music. Their impact lay in the political significance assigned to the sounds of the music or in the meaning of the words, or in both combined. If we turn to the significance of music itself as a means of communication, some of the arguments in favour of the political use of music can, in fact, be directed against it. In contrast to the view that music enhances a political message by presenting it in a pleasant and memorable way, and that it appeals more strongly to the emotions, it can be argued that, on the contrary, music detracts from any political message and deadens people's sensitivities. For example, in Ireland, although the content of popular music has often been political, I doubt if it has really contributed much to the freedom and well-being of the Irish people: it might even be said that the enjoyment of music has absorbed and sometimes fossilized 'revolutionary' zeal, and stifled political ingenuity, by containing frustration and anger in the rituals of song and dance.

This was the argument underlying Maurice Bloch's (1974) analysis of Merina religion which I mentioned in chapter 2. He argued that Merina political leaders used song and dance to reinforce traditional authority. Bloch contrasted the propositional force of ordinary language with the illocutionary or performative force of song, and concluded: 'In a song, therefore, no argument or reasoning can be communicated, no adaptation to the reality of the situation is possible.' Far from being superior forms of communication, song and dance are inferior forms of communication which anaesthetize the consciousness of all involved. This is a powerful argument, which rests very much on the redundancy and formal characteristics of song and dance as modes of communication. In so far as it is true in some societies, like that described by Bloch, it would apply as much to political song as to non-political song. That is, even a song with a strongly political text would be politically *in*effective simply because it used the anaesthetizing mode of musical communication.

I am sure that this is true in many societies, but it does not mean that music can never be politically effective. On the contrary, there are occasions when freedom of musical expression can not only express a desire for political freedom, but actually enhance political consciousness and push forward political action. In contrast to the situation described in Malagasy by Bloch, I have described (Blacking 1981) a situation in South Africa where music was used to articulate a desire for political freedom that could not easily be expressed in other ways. In South Africa in the 1960s, politics and music were inversely related to each other. Black South Africans could have stated in words ideas about political freedom, but they could not express them without almost certain imprisonment; on the other hand, they could not explain the significance of musical freedom in words, but they could, and did, express it in performance. The way in which members of some Independent Black South African churches sang, and much of the music that they sang, expressed opposition to white domination and reinforced the Africanist view of the political future of South Africa – a view which has come to the fore many times in South Africa's political history, but came to our notice most dramatically in the Black Consciousness and Black Theology movements of the 1970s and the Soweto uprising of 16 June 1976.

Members of the churches sang hymns of European origin very slowly, so as to allow for the maximum of individual ornamentation. It was a kind of democratic polyphony, whose musical structure was such that the conditions required for its performance generated feelings and relationships between people that enabled positive thinking and action in fields that were not musical. It was an aspect of the political role of music that I call 'the politics of music'. In such situations music comes into its own and is effective *as music*, and not merely because it refers to something else that is valued. When I talk of the role of music in politics, I refer to particular political situations that may be enhanced by music. In talking of the politics of music I may incidentally refer to particular political situations, but my chief concern is with the general political consequences of *musical* situations, the effects that music may have on the problems of people living and working together. In this case the actual performance of the music is a political event, whether or not it is recognized as such, and although different aspects of its structure may refer to or be derived from other features of the culture, the music as a whole is irreducible. Its performance is political in the sense that it may involve people in a powerful shared experience within the framework of their cultural experience and thereby make them more aware of themselves and of their responsibilities towards each other. Music is not then an escape from reality or a reinforcement of other political experiences: it is in itself an adventure into the reality of the sensuous and social capabilities of the species, and an experience of becoming in which individual consciousness is nurtured within the collective consciousness of the community.

The essence of a musical situation is that it is both formal and social, and that form and feeling are uniquely combined, and that it cannot be wholly successful as a form of communication unless it resonates with some universal human experiences as well as with the experiences of people in particular societies. People's self-feeling, which is essential for consciousness, for categorization and for all mental activity, is also their fellow-feeling, and just as reciprocal social interaction is a fact of the human condition, without which the brain could not begin to work as a human mind, so the form and content of the interaction both profoundly affect the ways in which the mind and body extend innate structures, and are able to generate new forms of experience. There is often a one-to-one relationship between the musical structure, the political content ('political' in the universal sense of relationships between humans and their fellow humans), and the effectiveness of music. Thus, for example, the most popular and politically important item of Venda traditional music, *tshikona*, has a musical structure that combines the maximum of individuality in community: at least twenty-five people perform in concert, and everyone does something different. African musical systems abound in examples of 'democratic polyphony', in which performance is also a political experience. In producing different kinds of sound, whether they involve voices, drums, pipes, xylophones, mbiras, or combinations of these timbres, many African societies prefer to create a performance situation that is not rational solely in terms of technical efficiency and economy of sound production, but rather generates reciprocal social interaction. Music that could be played by one person is shared amongst two, three, or more people, and the degree of social interaction required for performance enhances both individual and collective consciousness and generates greater human energy.

6

'The goal of musical progress': music as work or as leisure?

'IT AIN'T WHAT YOU DO, IT'S THE WAY THAT YOU DO IT'

Every weekday after my arrival in Australia, no matter how early I arrived in my room in the music department, or how late I left, I heard sounds that conjured up memories of a happy childhood in the 1930s. They recalled a routine of work, play, love, fellowship and worship, and confident talk of a future at school, university, and in one of the professions. The peace of my bourgeois existence was, in fact, an illusion, but the warmth and calm of my world had not been seriously disturbed by news of the Spanish Civil War or even the Munich Agreement.

The troubled European continent was a distant place, further away in my thoughts than some of the outposts of Commonwealth and Empire, which assumed importance in our school because of the careers they offered in colonial administration, farming, medicine, the army or police, and Christian missions. In 1937, two members of a group of German musicians stayed in our home whilst performing in the Salisbury district. They and their colleagues joined my father and friends in playing music for spinet, recorders, viols, and other Baroque instruments. We learnt after the war that some of our cheerful companions had been Nazis on a spying mission. In 1938, my grandmother began to be concerned for some of our Jewish relatives on the continent, and frequently urged me not to confuse Hitler's rantings with the sounds of a beautiful language and the music of a great cultural tradition.

Then came the War. But it did not shatter the complacency of my life. It rather added new dimensions, with the excitement of spotting enemy planes above the barrage balloons, the challenge of competing with school friends to design very fast

100

fighter-bombers, and the prospect of serving King and country in what seemed a worthwhile cause.

Children are not always psychologically scarred by war, especially if they can believe in what they are doing and in what is happening around them. Critics argued that Robert Westall's novel about wartime children, *The Machine Gunners* (1975), was absurdly far-fetched; but he was proved right by the flood of letters, photographs and reminiscences which readers sent him and which he later published in *Children of the Blitz* (1986).

War was compared to music in a British television serial on the Strauss family. After a destructive battle between the forces of the Emperor and the revolutionaries, Johann Strauss I replied to his wife's question, 'What was it all for?' with the words: 'It was like music. It wasn't for anything.' And yet music is at least for living, whereas the inevitable outcome of war must be that somebody dies or is damaged. War and music, like most human activities, are amoral and can be used for good or evil purposes. War can uplift or degrade people, depending on their attitudes towards the outcome of their actions, as Krishna pointed out to Arjuna in the *Bhagavad Gita*. We should remember that Krishna's pious remarks were made in the context of a caste system and a belief in reincarnation, and that Arjuna's destiny was prescribed by his being born a Kshatriya. It was not what people did, but how they did it that mattered.

The activities that we call 'the arts' are not intrinsically more ennobling, more worthy or more compassionate than sport, or cooking, or gardening. Perhaps tennis can be described as an art, as Joseph Mazo has described dance as a contact sport (Mazo 1974). I have seen lecturers in catering at the Manchester Polytechnic icing and decorating cakes as if they were sculptures. *The value of the arts in a society depends on how they are defined and used.* 'High art' is not intrinsically more worthy than 'low art', or music more valuable in itself than tennis or billiards. Music-making could be used as a front for spying. Some people can use sport like art to uplift a relationship and transcend harsh social realities, but appreciation of Beethoven's music did not restrain the jailers of Auschwitz.

The sounds that were music to my ears when I was in my room at the University of Western Australia were not the strains of the classics, or of Baroque or contemporary music, but the sounds of tennis balls. They evoked for me leisurely afternoons with my cousins on the lawn of the English country vicarage of West Lavington, Wiltshire, where one of my uncles worked. Once, during the 1939–45 War, those sounds were interrupted by my aunt's announcement that Charlie Montague's Armstrong Whitworth Whitley had been shot down over Germany; on another afternoon, the peaceful sound of tennis was punctuated by tense, repeated performances of *Country Gardens* on the drawing-room piano, as dished up by Percy Grainger for young ladies like my cousin Faith, who was preparing for a music examination.

Percy Grainger's music achieved for many people exactly what he hoped. It turned their minds away from the *Sturm und Drang* of Germanic composers and all the associated violence and torment of the European continent. It evoked and suited the English tennis parties, village fêtes, plus-fours and home-made clothing of the 1920s and 1930s, though it was tinged with a sadness that perhaps reflected the absence of friends, the underlying class conflict, and the displacement of violence to the colonies.

Percy Grainger understood his middle-class audience, but he seems to have misunderstood the period and its political implications. In 1934, he wrote in the twelfth of his broadcast lectures, 'The Goal of Musical Progress',

'Free music' (towards which all musical progress clearly points) will be the full musical expression of the scientific nature-worship begun by the Greeks and carried forward by the Nordic races. It will be the musical counterpart of Nordic pioneering, athleticism, nudism.

In all these respects it will be cosmic and impersonal, and thus fundamentally differentiated from the strongly personal and 'dramatic' music of non-Nordic Europe with its emphasis upon sex, possession, ambition, jealousy and strife.   (Appendix A:179–180)

I have deliberately quoted these curious statements, because they are typical of Grainger's contradictory views on many issues. He was convinced of the superiority of Nordic races and of blue-eyed composers; but he was also dedicated to a 'war' against German culture and music, and as early as 1919–21, he had openly supported Black Americans in their opposition to segregation and was giving 'his services free for concerts in aid of negro charities' (Bird 1976:166).

John Bird comments:

Perhaps the most curious aspect of Grainger was the fact that despite
the apparent inconsistencies of his thinking and the abnormalities
of his psychological make-up, he was, nevertheless, a man of total
integrity.   (Bird 1976:48)

To pile inconsistency upon inconsistency, it is essential to remember
that Grainger's relationships with people he loved were mostly marked
by a saintlike gentleness, sweetness and kindliness of nature. He seems
to have spent his life helping countless lame dogs over stiles. He was
generous beyond reason.   (Bird 1976:54)

It is not always clear how deeply he held some of his more crazy
notions and how much they were designed to shock and provoke,
and to exhibit a demonic and perverse streak in his character that
he felt was appropriate at that time to the public image of the
artist. I prefer to leave them aside and concentrate on the views
about music and society that he developed as a young man. They
were insightful, inspiring, and truly progressive.

Nevertheless, the 1934 lecture on the goal of musical progress revealed a major contradiction which may have inhibited
Grainger's work as he grew older. He seems to have seen musical
progress as depending on a new *style* of music, and on 'free
music' in particular. This contrasts sharply with his statement
that all the world should hear all the world's music, in which
he was concerned to promote a new outlook on music-making,
a new way of using music in society. A transformation of musical
life in industrial societies was and still is needed, and Grainger
saw this very clearly as a young man. Musical progress could
not be achieved simply by changes in musical form. There
had to be changes in the ways that music was made. In 1915,
Percy Grainger argued, in effect, that the value of music had
been debased because of the ways in which music-making and
musicians were defined and used:

With regard to music, our modern Western civilization produces, broadly
speaking, two main types of educated men. On the one hand the
professional musician or leisured amateur-enthusiast who spends the
bulk of his waking hours making music, and on the other hand all those
many millions of men and women whose lives are far too overworked
and arduous, or too completely immersed in the ambitions and
labyrinths of our material civilization, to be able to devote any reasonable
proportion of their time to music or artistic expression of any kind at

all. How different from either of these types is the bulk of uneducated and 'uncivilized' humanity of every race and colour, with whom natural musical expression may be said to be a universal, highly prized habit that seldom, if ever, degenerates into the drudgery of a mere means of livelihood.   (Balough 1982:66)

Under the subheading 'The tyranny of the composer', he wrote:

The fact that art-music has been written down instead of improvised has divided musical creators and executants into two quite separate classes; the former autocratic and the latter comparatively slavish...though the state of things obtaining among trained musicians for several centuries has been productive of isolated geniuses of an exceptional greatness unthinkable under primitive conditions, it seems to me that it has done so at the expense of the artistry of millions of performers.
                                                 (Balough 1982:74)

Grainger was convinced that the division of labour between composer, performer, and listener was not only unnatural, but also unnecessary and inimical to the general use of music as the basis of a rich, personal life, which I discussed in chapter 2.

In response to the objection that music-making is available only to a chosen few, he argued that the complexity of folk music was evidence of a natural propensity for 'artistic self-expression'. He also insisted that

mental leisure and ample opportunity for indulging in [this] natural instinct...are the conditions imperative for the production and con-tinuance of all unwritten music. Now primitive modes of living, however terrible some of them may appear to some educated and refined people, are seldom so barren of 'mental leisure' as the bulk of our civilized careers. The old, ignorant, unambitious, English yokel, for instance, had plenty of opportunities for giving way to his passion for singing.   (Balough 1982:66–7)

Not only does the commercial slavery of our civilization hold out to the average man insufficient leisure for the normal growth of the habit of artistic expression (unless he shows talents *exceptional* enough to warrant becoming a professional artist) but the many decorums of modern society deny to most of us any very generous opportunities for using even our various (unartistic) life-instincts to the full.
                                              (*ibid.*, italics in original)

In other words, all human beings have a right to music and the opportunity of artistic expression, and therefore the goal of musical progress must be not so much to create 'free music', as to enable free people to be free to make music. *The value of the arts in a society depends on how they are defined and used.*

In their traditional musical system, the Venda of Southern Africa distinguished between communal music and individual instrumental music and songs. Communal music was broadly divided into 'play' music (*mitambo*), which was mostly for young people, and ritual music (*ngoma*). Beer-songs, whose performance occupied a great deal of adult spare time, were neither play nor ritual, but they were used as often for interfamily rituals as they were for general entertainment after work, which itself was accompanied by work songs whenever communal labour was organized. There were subdivisions of genre according to the institutions that the music accompanied, but there were no obvious musical distinctions between ritual and play music. Whether play music was performed slightly differently and incorporated in ritual music, or whether it was performed in its own right, it was no less serious than ritual music. The categories were related to the political implications of the music, rather than to any underlying concepts of work and leisure. Play music could be just as much hard work as ritual music, as when girls and boys rehearsed for several weeks to go on a musical expedition to another district (Blacking 1962).

If the Venda performed communal music chiefly when their stomachs were full, it was not simply to pass time. Co-operative and inventive behaviour could not be overlooked in the pursuit of self-preservation, or the harmony of nature would have been disturbed. People could not be satisfied with having: they must also be, and become. But nor could they be, without having. When the Venda were hungry, or busy working to avoid hunger, they did not have the time or energy to make much music except work-songs. Nor did they imagine that music might in some magical way alleviate their hunger, any more than their rain-makers expected rain to fall before they saw the insects whose movements preceded it. The music was always in them, but it required special conditions to emerge. The Venda made music when their stomachs were full, not because music was a leisure activity, but because they sensed the forces of alienation inherent in their acts of material production, which were artefacts of cultural history, and music-making was the work that helped them to restore the balance with exceptionally co-operative and inventive behaviour. Their use of the concept of work (*mushumo*) was not limited to material production. Nights spent in prayer and hymn-singing were described as *mushumo wa Mudzimu* (work for God), and Venda Christians tended to take a rather poor view of the leisurely way in which Europeans went about their religious worship, and indeed their social relations.

In 1915, Percy Grainger showed that he was more aware than many music educators, even in 1985, of the lessons that can be learnt from the ways in which unwritten music was and is used in societies like Venda.

If there again should dawn an age in which the bulk of civilized men and women will come to again possess sufficient mental leisure in their lives to enable them to devote themselves to artistic pleasures on so large a scale as do the members of uncivilized communities...Then the spectacle of one composer producing music for thousands of musical drones... will no longer seem normal or desirable, and then the present gulf between the mentality of composers and performers will be bridged.

(Balough 1982:74)

Although Percy Grainger sometimes called himself a socialist and was much impressed by George Bernard Shaw's lectures (Bird 1976:70), I have found no reference to his having read or discussed Karl Marx's views on art. And yet his statements are very similar to the points which Marx made about the role of the senses in the 1844 *Economic and Philosophical Manuscripts*. The main difference is that Grainger argued, rightly in my opinion, that there had been a time when art encroached upon life and that it could still be observed in some societies, whereas Karl Marx expressed the hope that it would emerge in the future.

In an article entitled, 'Is there a theory of art in Marx?', Hans Hess (1973) argued that Marx had failed to see that the consumption or reception of art, as well as its production, was historically 'bound up with certain forms of social development'. Thus 'modern admiration for Greek art owed less to some trans-historical essence in the works themselves than to the aesthetic ideologies or philosophies prevailing in modern societies and their corresponding cultural institutions' (Laing 1978:11). 'Marx did not see that it was not the same thing which had survived, it had lost its content, only the form remained – beautiful as it was' (Hess 1973:311).

Even so, Hess showed that 'Marx actually knew that art forms, especially when re-used, are ideological disguises' (*ibid.*): in a letter to Lassalle of 22 July 1861, four years after he wrote his comments on Greek art, Marx 'acknowledged the survival of artistic forms in a context where their use or meaning had changed' (Laing 1978:11). This general principle has been proved correct again and again, but I take issue with the notion that 'in the first instance, the work of art honestly proclaims its ideological message', whilst 'in its survival state, the original becomes a fake and a prop of what Marx calls: "false consciousness"' (Hess 1973:311).

Firstly, at least as far as the performing arts are concerned, I see no reason why the change of meaning should become a 'misinterpreted' form, rather than a re-interpretation. This was the point I was arguing about different versions of Beethoven's 'Hammerklavier' Sonata and will also make about so-called 'authentic' performances of Baroque and other ancient musics (cf. pp. 19 and 125). It was also the theme of Ruth Katz's study of changing mannerisms in the singing of Aleppo Jews (p. 47). And Joann Keali'inohomoku has shown how the Hawai'ian hula was functionally related to the old religion, the old technology, the old hierarchical political system, and many other features of pre-contact Hawai'i which Hawai'ians do not wish to revive. But it has become viable again through a re-interpretation of the hula which fulfils the Hawai'ian need to maintain a sense of cultural identity in the context of contemporary Hawai'ian society (Keali'inohomoku 1979).

Secondly, the 'reception' of artistic 'messages' depends not so much on their intended content and how they are proclaimed, as on how performers, audiences and spectators make sense of them. People do not simply react to art with culturally and socially conditioned responses: they make artistic sense of certain phenomena in the world, as Percy Grainger often emphasized (e.g. pp. 44–5). Just as performers and audiences create a work of music every time they perform it, so critics and readers become participants in the works they read (see Hawkes 1977:157). No readings of a work are 'wrong, they all add to the work' (Hawkes, *ibid.*); a work 'is eternal not because it imposes a single meaning on different men, but because it suggests different meanings to a single man' (Roland Barthes, quoted in Hawkes 1977). Thus

Arnold Kettle did not find it incompatible with his socialism to argue that looking back to the great literary products of the bourgeois world and recognizing their place in human evolution was part of the task of inventing the future (Kettle 1972).

Hess summed up Marx's arguments as he interpreted them from statements in *Economic and Philosophical Manuscripts*, *Grundrisse* and *The German Ideology*. Art provided the means by which human beings could attain ownership of the senses and overcome the alienation from their true essence. In the communist society of the future, '*the* artist' as a special category will be redundant, all men and women will cultivate their artistic capabilities, and there will be no more painters but only men and women who also paint. The distinction between producer and consumer of art will abolish itself, and art and life will become one.

Percy Grainger drew attention to the fact that in some societies and communities art and life were already one, and that aesthetic experience and artistic modes of cognition could be, and had been historically, primary modelling systems for living. Thus art can be seen not as the products of certain kinds of human labour in 'free time' but as a *process* (cf. pp. 24–5 above) by which all labour and social interaction can be transformed; and the development of the senses can be seen not as the result of *any* kind of social labour (cf. Marx in Fromm 1961:134), but more specifically, of artistic labour in particular.

'RAT RACE'

'Oh! It's a disgrace
To see the human race
In the rat race'   (Bob Marley)

Musical progress cannnot be separated from political progress, nor political freedom from musical freedom. And just as political freedom is not a corollary of high technology or a notable characteristic of technologically advanced societies, so musical progress cannot be measured in terms of technical complexity. Mastery of technique has never been more than a means to an end except for the most tawdry of composers. The argument that music must be highly technical in a scientific age is as silly as saying that computerized police records of the lives of a country's citizens are the best way of guaranteeing individual freedom. Political awareness is innate, but it can be quickly lost as children become progressively institutionalized and lose that capacity to monitor every social situation and carefully adjust and manipulate the balance of power. Similarly, artistic capacities are innate, and enable children to feel, to express, to explore, to invent, and to stretch their bodies.

In 1982, when my daughter Thalia was just four years old and beginning at school, she made a remark that was similar to the Balinese adage: 'We have no art; we do everything as well as we can.' When asked what she wanted to do in life, she said 'I want to be a famous everything'. Asked to elaborate, she said that she wanted to be famous in all the things she did. After a year's schooling, she modified this expression of transcendent joy in life with a cautious, deflated, culturally conditioned remark: when she heard me tell a friend that she was going to be a famous everything, she interjected, 'No I'm not! I'm not going to be a famous everything anymore.' Now I certainly do not wish my children to have a separate, artistic education and become like those ghoulish, egocentric youths in the television series *Fame*; but on the other hand, I don't want their formal schooling to constrain their political and artistic development.

In any case, whatever their educational experience, musicians are subject to all kinds of pressures on their work. Although Percy Grainger, like Bertrand Russell and many other creative people, gained much by being educated privately, his artistic expression was later constrained by the pattern of professional life and the economics of the performing arts, and particularly by the presence of his mother, who became his exclusive business manager and had to be supported by his earnings. He became a victim of the political economy that produces *Fame*, and of the contradictions that enable David Bowie to turn down an offer of a million American dollars for a few minutes' work – more than Bach and Mozart together earned for their lives' work.

I realize that we are living in a world where the leisure activities of my childhood have become sources of huge incomes for a few committed, hard-working individuals, and that those working on the University tennis courts could earn much more than those in the music department's studios. I also appreciate that tennis can be as artistic as music and, although I admire David Bowie's work, I think that he is far less skilled as a musician than are

Bjorn Borg and Martina Navratilova as tennis players. On the other hand David Bowie, like Bob Marley, and the minstrels of traditional African societies whose work seemed to be *less* musical than that of other musicians, is political and rather subversive, but Bjorn Borg and Martina Navratilova are not. He is playing the capitalist game, but he is also undermining our highly materialistic, capitalistic, political structures, just as the elitism of Russian musicians and Russian musical life is exposing the contradictions of Russian socialism. The absurdity of David Bowie's earnings in relation to the general pattern of economic life of his society shows clearly that market forces have nothing to do with the welfare and freedom of individual citizens; similarly, the special education of talented Soviet artists and athletes, and the pampered treatment that they receive, fly in the face of Marx's arguments about the place of the arts and the abolition of '*the* artist' in a socialist society, and merely ape patterns of life of capitalist modes of production.

If we want to evaluate the evolutionary status of a society and measure its health and creative potential, perhaps we should look, not to its balance of payments, the wealth of its elite, or its military power, but to the state of its collective life and the ways in which it is using artistic processes to cultivate *all* its citizens' ownership of the senses and promote their individual freedom, and to develop its power of mind and its social and cultural coherence.

Percy Grainger was right when he declared that 'the commercial slavery of our civilization' is inimical to the progress of artistic life and the development of human potential and individual freedom. Technologically advanced societies, capitalist and socialist alike, need to organize their musical (and general artistic) life so that art encroaches upon life. In the third and fourth chapter on the origins of musical ideas, I gave some of the reasons why this is necessary for the survival of the human species.

Thus, *the value of the arts in a society depends on how they are defined and used*, but there are certain values that can transcend the ways in which a society organizes its artistic life because of the forces that are at work in every human body, and especially the motivation to grow and extend the body, and hence to use the powers of the two hemispheres of the brain complementarily.

It is this 'growth-motivation' or need for 'self-actualization', as Rogers and Maslow have called it (Maslow 1954), which drives people to co-operate and stretch their intellectual powers. Above all, it constantly resurrects the force of affect and nonverbal modes of communication, which are characteristically associated with the activity of the right hemisphere of the brain and by which human beings *feel* their way towards new relationships, new ideas, and new social formations, and so overcome the alienation that far from perfect social and cultural systems have brought on them. 'We feel before we understand', said the Ghanaian musician, Papa Oyeah MacKenzie,[17] in describing the role of affective culture in transforming human lives.

ETHNOMUSICOLOGICAL DIALECTIC AND MUSICAL PROGRESS

A major task of ethnomusicology is to assess the status of music and musical activity in a society at any given time and to be able to recommend how music can most usefully be used to achieve certain ends. I am not suggesting that ethnomusicologists can or should play God; but I do claim that because of their study of different musical systems in different social and cultural contexts, they can sometimes have privileged access to understanding the implications of a musical situation more clearly than those who are involved in it. Their task is then not to tell people what to do, but to engage in dialectic that enables those involved to work out a number of possible solutions.

There are two recent studies which illustrate rather well the kind of dialectic in which ethnomusicologists can usefully engage. The first is theoretical and the second practical. Steve Feld analysed relationships between sound, sentiment, birds, water, poetics and weeping amongst the Kaluli of the highlands of Papua New Guinea (Feld 1982). This followed on from studies such as my own among the Venda and Hugo Zemp's among the 'Are'are of the Solomon Islands in giving an account of an indigenous ethno-theory of musical communication. Feld spent much time asking questions of musicians and arguing with them about how they conceptualized what they were doing and feeling. He produced a very rich study of the coherence of people's ideas, social life and affective culture. But I suggest that it was more

a *product of dialectic* between practising musicians and an
analytical ethnomusicologist, than a record of received wisdom.
Although I am sure that many Kaluli informants had thought
much about their music before Feld arrived, and they clearly
had a system of categorization and a theory of communication,
I doubt if they had produced such an elaborate exegesis before
they had the intellectual challenge from the visiting ethnomusicologist. One might say the same about dialogues with
composers, such as Robert Craft's conversations with Stravinsky.

It is difficult to assess the musical or social consequences
of these kinds of activity. Malinowski's brilliant studies of
Trobriand society and culture have had more impact in Europe
and North America than in Papua New Guinea, and Feld's
analysis of Kaluli music really has more immediate implications
for academic music theory and music education than it does for
the future of a tiny community in a rapidly developing nation.
Even though artistic activity may be a prime factor in social life,
it is unreasonable to expect developing countries to place the
arts high on their agenda for research and funding, when most
developed industrial nations treat them as a luxury of secondary
importance.

It was therefore all the more remarkable that the Tanzanian
government should appreciate the importance of an ethnomusicological study as part of a multi-disciplinary project in-
volving the Tanzanian Ministry of Culture and Development, the
Government of Finland and the University of Helsinki's Department of Development Studies, and the villagers of the Bagamoyo
district. Their task was to carry out field research and draw up
plans for the district's future development. Philip Donner was
the ethnomusicologist in charge of research into music and
dance, and he proposed that *ngoma ya selo*, the most important
regional dance, should be developed and more widely used as a
means of extending consciousness and promoting artistic skills
(Donner 1981). There is, however, a perennial problem in using
traditional art forms as vital parts of programmes of social and
technological change: unless they are *socially* reconstructed as
well as technically developed, their use can hold back, rather than
enhance, change. Wider use of *ngoma ya selo* alone, for example,
would be unlikely to expand social consciousness, especially if
there were no change in the roles of performers. But if women

could assume men's traditional musical and choreographic roles, and vice versa, the focus of experience might be shifted from the *social* use of music to the politics of *music* as a transforming force. Secondly, if those for whom *ngoma ya selo* was the appropriate regional music were to perform music from other areas, and others added *ngoma ya selo* to their repertoire, this sharing of regional musical styles could enhance the wider consciousness that was considered necessary for Tanzania's national development. Subsequent developments of music and dance training in Bagamoyo, guided by Mr Martin Buriani, have in fact been immensely fruitful; and young amateur musicians have performed abroad with great success, as well as contributed to the growth of national consciousness.

In Zambia, the national dance group is made up of people from many parts of the country, so that all members, for example, sing, play, and perform dances from different sub-cultures, which they were usually taught by people who were brought up in those areas. Thus regional styles acquire national significance, just as in Europe national composers have acquired international significance.

Many African nations face two sets of problems that are posed by (1) the variety of indigenous cultures and the fact that, because of patterns of colonial development, some are more prominent nationally than others, and (2) the apparent discrepancy between standards of training required for excellence in the indigenous arts and in those styles that have been imported from outside.

Careful analyses of traditional African styles of music and dance, such as Drs Akin Euba's (1974) and Joshua Uzoigwe's (1981) studies of Nigerian *dundun* and *ukom* musics, invariably reveal that excellence of performance in many genres requires no less training or attention to detail than study of the violin or the piano in a European conservatory. Ghana, Nigeria, Kenya, and Uganda are four of many African states where students pursue serious training in styles of traditional music and dance along with their study of European instruments and techniques. Bi-musicality is becoming necessary for anyone who wishes to obtain a music degree at an African university, and the contact of sophisticated urban students with master-musicians and dancers who often come from rural areas helps to increase their respect for indigenous traditions and those who have been carrying them.

Solutions need to be found for communal music-making and dancing in education and in the community, so that some indigenous musics and dances are not promoted to the exclusion of others and the experience of performance can be separated from any specific, and inevitably local, social context.

Of all aspects of culture, affective culture is most likely to transcend changing social formations. But while it may remain formally static it can be socially and emotionally dynamic, so that there need not be contradictions between the development of a nation and the perpetuation of its artistic forms. If restructuring of rural communities is needed as a necessary step in socialist reconstruction, an initial change of roles for music-making could prepare people for subsequent social changes. Similarly, the reality of new political groupings can be most effectively experienced when people perform together music that symbolizes those new groups. In the past, groups of Venda organized themselves for music-making before they used their musical organization as a base for other, non-musical activities.

I am not suggesting that the sounds of music should drown the cries of the poor, the needy, the sick and the alienated: on the contrary, the patterns of social interaction and the experiences engendered by musical performances should help to develop the senses and raise consciousness, so that people can take control of their own destiny, improve their lot, and together create communities that are truly independent of foreign exploitation and interests that seek to undermine their integrity.

The new Academies of Performing Arts which are springing up in different parts of the world could have profound effects on the social and economic development of their countries, provided that they manage to maintain a balance between the extremes of cultivating professional elites of artists of world standard, and training dedicated teachers who will be able to promote the performing arts in colleges, schools, and community centres. Similarly, these academies might well differ from existing institutions in offering a broader syllabus.

Firstly, they could emphasize *world* music, dance and drama, with special attention to indigenous art forms. This is a trend that is being adopted increasingly by progressive academies and departments in many parts of the world. Secondly, they could encourage communal participation in artistic practice, to improve the quality of life, enhance general educational performance, and to become directly involved in therapy and remedial education. Thirdly, they could provide back-up skills for the arts, by training instrument and other technicians. Any increase in musical life will require an increase in able technicians. We should not forget that many composers, such as Purcell, earned a living primarily as Keepers of Instruments.

When the Royal College of Music was set up in London on 28 February 1882 (cf. Ehrlich 1985:107–16), England was known as *'Das Land ohne Musik'*, the land without music. This was not, in fact, true: there was a great deal of music-making in the home, in churches and in chapels, and there were many brass bands and community choirs in the new industrial towns of the North, quite apart from a widespread and vigorous tradition of folk-song. There was therefore plenty of music-making as there is in many parts of the world today, but the pool of talent was not developed and it seemed to outsiders that there was nothing to show for it in the way of internationally known artists and composers.

The Royal Academy of Music had been founded in London sixty years earlier, but formal music education had not been easily available to all. The founding of the Royal College was a popular cause that was achieved with the co-operation of all classes, and the Prince of Wales, at the public opening in 1883, said that he hoped the College would 'bridge over the gulf between different classes which it is the tendency of increased wealth and increased civilization to widen'. *The Times* of 8 May 1883 reported that among the first fifty scholars 'a mill girl, the daughter of a brickmaker, and the son of a blacksmith take high places in singing, while the son of a farm labourer excels in violin playing'.

I mention this for three reasons: first, academies that give opportunities for the poorest citizens will touch the hearts of the finest musicians in Europe and North America so that they will not have difficulties in recruiting good teachers; second, it will be necessary to be flexible about entrance requirements – none of those poor, talented scholars of the Royal College of Music could have passed the array of exams which now hamper the musical development of young people; and third, the 'new life for English music' which the College helped to produce also held out hopes of a new life and new career opportunities for many young Englishmen and women whose lives and talents would have otherwise remained unfulfilled.

Another attractive feature of some new Academies of Performing Arts, and especially that in Hong Kong which was opened in 1985, is their inclusion of more than one of the performing arts. The re-integration of the performing arts is already becoming a fact of life in industrial societies, and of great interest to many composers, choreographers and dramatists, just as it remains the predominant feature of the major traditional art forms of Asia and Africa. It is necessary to break down entrenched divisions of labour in the arts that had until recently tended to restrict artistic experience and imagination in Europe and America, so that people may learn to relate art forms not only to each other but also to other aspects of social reality.

One of the major barriers to the development of the performing arts as an integral part of social life and as special kinds of social activity that absorb and unite mind, body, emotion and reason, is that they demand considerable technical skills without which people are not really free to communicate with each other. The pressures of modern technical education and the proliferation of other methods of filling spare time, such as sport and television, have greatly reduced people's incentives to cultivate artistic skills, so that, for example, the domestic and community music-making that formed the infrastructure of German musical life, and the amateur dramatic societies that whetted English people's appetites for drama, have lost their appeal. Paradoxically, the formalization of arts training and the proliferation of examinations have frequently had the opposite effect of turning young people *away from* the performing arts at the very time when they are well disposed to practice them assiduously.

For example, at the age of eight my daughter Leila practised horse-riding skills with monotonous regularity because of the constantly dynamic relationship with the horses she rides; she practised the piano because she liked her teacher and was given new pieces to learn; she did her homework because she usually found it new and interesting; but she was bored with dancing and gave it up, because there was endless repetition of the same movements and no real interaction with class-mates or teacher, whose concern was to prepare pupils for their examinations.

The reaction of many parents to such a situation would be to conclude that their child is too bright at school work to waste time dancing, that dancers think with their feet, and so on. On the other hand, there is evidence that the experience of imaginative dance classes significantly enhances the academic performance of many children in poor areas of Liverpool (Linton 1984); and the Hungarian music educationist, Dr Klara Kokas, and her colleagues have established that the creativity of culturally deprived children in Boston and in some Hungarian schools was greatly improved by regular musical performance (Barkóczi and Pléh 1982).

The point I want to make is this: can we organize training in the performing arts in such a way that skills may be acquired more quickly and effectively, and children can early acquire the magical, as well as the social, experience of performance that will enable them to forge ahead without being disheartened?

Innovation in pedagogy could be enhanced by exploring the effectiveness of methods that have been used in other traditions, as well as the different idioms in which the skills are learnt. For instance, Balinese girls perform dance movements of a kind that my daughter's teacher would consider too advanced for her even at a later age; and Venda children sang hexatonic and heptatonic melodies and played polyrhythms at a stage when Western pedagogues consider they should be singing pentatonic melodies with isorhythms.

Perhaps we can find ways of producing good performers more quickly than in the past, and more effective ways of learning can be devised, as they have been for language and other skills. Perhaps switching from one performance tradition to another, as children often do for language in a bilingual environment, may speed up the learning of both traditions. Perhaps some development of the Suzuki method, with family involvement and the abolition of restrictive exams, may help learning at all stages. The application of such principles of learning will ultimately have to take place long before most children are old enough to enter an academy.

Artistic growth and economic growth are different phenomena. The arts are not primarily a commodity to be manufactured and exported for entertainment, but a plant to be grown, tended, and contemplated for the sake of individual spiritual development and the enhancement of relations with others.

THE POWER OF MUSIC

The development of the senses and the education of the emotions through the arts are not merely desirable options. They are essential both for balanced action and the effective use of the intellect. Obviously, music will always be on sale in the market-place, and there may continue to be professionals. But the important developments of the future must be in the restoration of the masses' right to musical experience and the cultivation of excellence, and also in the re-integration of the arts.

The division of labour was an important stage in the development of technology, communication, and larger societies of human beings. Its original purpose was to improve human welfare, but it became a source of exploitation as well as of some remarkable cultural products. The separation of musical styles and the organization of musical life into work for some and leisure for others, are reflections of the division of labour in industrial societies. But artistic activities are not meant to mirror false consciousness: they should rather combat it by liberating human awareness. Thus in a society like the United Kingdom, which has been torn apart by the inequalities of wealth and power that have arisen from abuses of the technological division of labour, abolition of a division of labour in music and the arts can be an important first step towards the restoration of conscious-ness and of ownership of the senses, and the creation of the more egalitarian society that is necessary if we are to survive some of the imminent perils of the 1980s and 1990s and move confidently into the twenty-first century.

With the development of high technology, material production can be achieved with fewer people and fewer working hours, so that concepts of work and leisure have to be readjusted. The traditional academic curriculum has been built round and justified by the notion of preparing people for materially productive labour for five or six days of the week and forty years of life. As we move back to the three- or four-day working week which was the norm in the majority of pre-industrial societies, we must use the other two or three days as days for other kinds of work, and therefore incorporate those work activities into the curriculum. Moreover, changes in technology need not create unemployment or leisure time, so much as time for other kinds of artistic work. For example, a reduction in time spent on producing printed material allows for care and craftsmanship to be devoted once more to the production of books in which the medium of communication is a work of art as much as, or even more than, its contents.

Expansion of markets for the arts must depend on education and not on state patronage. The kind of state patronage proposed in the report of the British Labour Party's Study Group on the Arts (1975), for instance, would only contribute to the maintenance of an artistic elite. It was concerned more with society's obligations to 'the artist' than its responsibilities to itself, and it would perpetuate class divisions and give the ruling classes the monopoly of the arts, rather than enable artistic practice to become the common property of society as a whole. Besides, if we are going to select some people to be artists and superstars and treat the arts as a luxury, then music will have to be increasingly subsidized and patronized, and the aim of promoting musical appreciation and activity in all sections of society could not be realized without astronomical public expense.

There is a case for subsidizing the arts and professional artists within the sphere of education; but there is no good reason for paying a singer or a conductor more than a senior civil servant when a performance is supported by public funds – even if their names are Sutherland or von Karajan. If a composer of operas cannot make the same sort of living as a composer of musical comedies, does he/she have a right to a special subsidy simply because a certain class of society considers opera to have more value than musical comedy?

Bach was employed as a teacher and found time to compose in between fulfilling his task as a teacher. There is no evidence that exclusive attention to artistic creation as a full-time occupation significantly improves the quality or quantity of an artist's output.

On economic grounds, then, it can be argued that the only legitimate outlet for state support of the arts is in and through education, and that any other form of state patronage will only increase the need for further and more expensive patronage. Increasing public expense on the arts could perhaps be justified if it could be shown that this would benefit larger numbers of people. But, in fact, the majority of the United Kingdom's tax-paying population enjoy arts that are provided by private enterprise on a profit and loss basis (e.g. pop and rock concerts), and the subsidized arts (e.g. Covent Garden) benefit comparatively few members of society, most of whom could easily afford more expensive seats.

In 1976, the Maud report on *Support for the Arts* concluded that:

The long-term future of artists is in the hands of educators. The lead given since the war by a minority of schools, colleges, teachers and education authorities must now be followed by the rest. Our children and grandchildren must have, at all stages of their education, the chance of acquiring arts and habits not only of reading, writing and mathematics but of discrimination and creative action – of making music, writing poetry and plays, acting and dancing, designing and applying creative skills.

For these things to happen a revolution is needed in the curriculum and teaching methods of the great majority of schools and colleges of education.   (Redcliffe-Maud 1976:51)

This is marvellous. But a revolution in the curriculum is unlikely to occur until there has been a revolution in our thinking about the arts and artists. The idea that educationalists must be converted 'to the belief that arts are as important to society as reading, writing and arithmetic, not a disposable extra' (Redcliffe-Maud 1976:52) will not carry conviction as long as people maintain the defeatist, elitist notion that artistic talent is a 'rare gift' (Redcliffe-Maud 1976:54).

Ethnomusicological research has shown that there is no longer any justification for such an attitude to musical talent. The goal of musical progress in a country should not be more education for a special class of musicians, but the musical education and sensory liberation of the majority of citizens. Musical praxis has the power to do more than reflect social formations and integrate people's experience of their feelings about them: it can help to generate new ideas and experiences that could be applied in any field of social life. Music is like the laser in the early 1960s: it is a solution in search of problems. Its potential for transforming the lives of people in industrial societies has yet to be explored.

'Let all the world hear all the world's music': popular music-making and music education

UNDERSTANDING MUSIC THROUGH PERFORMANCE

The gramophone and the tape-recorder arrived on the music scene just in time to save art music from becoming fossilized. I refer not so much to the new worlds of sound that have been made available to composers through recordings of exotic music from Asia, Africa, the Caribbean, Eastern Europe, and Latin America, as to the growing emphasis on performance and varieties of interpretation. This has been the inevitable result of having many recordings of the same written work.

The tape-recorder has abolished what had been seen as the essential differences between written and unwritten music. Recordings of unwritten music have revealed that it is much less improvised and more stable and systematic than had previously been thought; and recorded interpretations of written music have shown that even for the most scholarly and careful performers, the score is only an approximate guide to performance. Just as multiple performances of a Beethoven symphony show that there are as many readings as there are orchestras and conductors, so recordings of apparently improvised African music reveal a consistency of performance which suggests that the musicians hold in their heads both the grammar of a musical system and the equivalent of a musical score.

Thus the *making* of the music, the element that was so important in the time of Bach when people worked from a figured bass, or in Mozart's and Beethoven's time when soloists improvised cadenzas on the spur of the moment, the *act of performance*, has come into its own once more.

The invention which allows us to avoid going to symphony

concerts, and which in a sense reduced the need for live performances, brings music more alive by encouraging careful listening.
Recordings can make us more conscious of the *music* that is being
played, because we can listen in intimate surroundings without
the interference of external elements. The availability of multiple
recordings of works allows us to dissent from local fashion and
develop our personal tastes in composers and performances.

It is perhaps no coincidence that greater opportunities for
listening to the music and making intelligent judgements about
sonorities have coincided with a period in music-making in
which exceptional emphasis is laid on timbre and sound quality.
This applies as much to composition and arrangements of pop
and rock music as it does to contemporary 'art' music and the
discovery of folk and traditional music from all parts of the world.
The invention of the gramophone and tape-recorder, as well as
the radio, have helped to detach music from social class, time,
place, and the limits of specific musical instruments. People can
now turn on almost any music they like at any time of day or
night, and composers can conjure up with tape and synthesizers
whatever sounds they imagine.

Timbre has always been an important ingredient of style, if
only because it is the most obvious parameter that immediately
distinguishes even different uses of the same instrumental
ensemble (cf. the quartet sounds of Beethoven and Brahms and
the contrasting sounds of different rock groups). But it has also
been given a rather static quality as a symbol of social boundaries
and social function. For instance, it is hard to hear the sounds of
a brass band, an organ, a hymn, a gamelan, a saxophone or a sitar,
without associating them with particular kinds of people, places,
and events. Similarly, many African Christians have rarely
incorporated drums into their religious music, even if they are
shaped and played in European style, because they cannot
dissociate the musical sound from the appropriate pagan practices
and social groups.

Because it can be detached from specific social functions,
times and places, recorded music permits freer exploration of
sonorities, without the restrictions of social convention. I know
of the son of a professional academic musician who turned
against the 'art' music of the eighteenth, nineteenth, and early
twentieth centuries and became deeply involved in the world of

pop, rock, and jazz as part of the social process of developing teenage identity. He became fascinated by the varieties of timbre, and this interest in sonorities led him to the world of contemporary 'art' music, and subsequently on to the kinds of 'art' music which he had earlier rejected.

This anecdote recalls a general principle of musical experience which I mentioned in earlier chapters and which has been brought into prominence by the inventions of the gramophone and the tape-recorder, and the consequential increase of available musical variety and of audiences to hear it: *it does not matter so much what music you hear as how you listen to it, and how it is performed.* The aesthetic value of music does not lie in any objective product but in the subjective processes of composing, performing, and listening to the music. Music, like all art-objects, is available-for-use; and the essence of the artistic process is that it must be exercised as much by performers and listeners as by the original creators.

Thus a work of art may be performed and heard inartistically; or a mundane object may be transformed into a work of art by an enthusiastic buyer or viewer. The art is in the making, and we cannot dismiss as non-art a Tretchikoff print if it ennobles the vision and sharpens the sensitivities of a Belfast dock worker.

The evidence for this view of art and the artistic process is overwhelming, but people still hold to the old argument that absolute judgements can be made about music, claiming that some music is art, while other music is not, and that certain kinds or items of music are better than others. People who make such judgements often confuse music sound with its social origins and environment, and try to invest purely personal preference with a measure of objectivity and authority. If this were not so, how could Spohr have been honoured as one of the twelve great composers by the builders of the Chicago Symphony Hall in the late nineteenth century? And how could the music of Mahler have been unappreciated by the educated and sensitive ears of his contemporaries? The point is that musical performances are multi-media events, and their sound patterns are but one of several channels of communication. Listening is therefore influenced by fashion, changing social values, personal whim, and experiences of enculturation. The circumstances surrounding the presentation of Spohr's music in the late nineteenth century were presumably better for its enthusiastic reception than those surrounding performances of Mahler's music in the early twentieth century.

In most human interaction, several channels of communication are working simultaneously. Consider, for example, verbal language: its syntax is accompanied by patterns of posture, gesture, intonation, costume, social environment, and other modes of communication which can alter the message even when there is no change of code. Not all channels are noted or labelled by the actors, but this does not mean that the labelled are valued more highly or perceived more keenly than the unlabelled. Thus, people may talk about musical experience in political or religious terms, but this does not necessarily mean that they do not hear or enjoy the music as 'form in tonal motion', or that they regard it as subordinate to political and religious issues. On the contrary, the music may express more precisely than any political or religious dogma the really important values that underlie a person's political or religious commitment, such as a sense of human brotherhood or a desire to worship.

Similarly, it is too easy to explain a pop festival in purely sociological terms and to ignore its significance as a musical event. It may indeed be a case of commercial exploitation, a social gathering, an assertion of youthful identity and revolt, an opportunity for sexual and narcotic exchange, or whatever; but it can also be an occasion on which people respond to musical ideas and achieve some degree of transcendence. The opposite can also occur: people can talk in learned and ecstatic terms about musical forms, and yet be much more concerned with their status vis-à-vis other concert-goers, colleagues and friends, and their self-importance as 'cultured' beings.

Whether people can recognize a tune by the Beatles or by Beethoven is simply a matter of degree and a consequence of social experience. What is more important is that most people can distinguish the parameters of musical modes of communication from linguistic, gestural, and other modes, although they may not be able to explain what they do in words. When I speak of 'understanding music through performance', I mean by the word 'performance' both the physical involvement of performance and the experience of remaking music by listening. Recorded music provides unparalleled opportunities for reflection, which

can only lead to better understanding of music and richer cultivation of people's musicality.

Let me take another analogy from verbal language. Understanding a verbal language precedes the ability to perform, as we
know very well from infants' frustrated attempts to reciprocate
the messages that they receive from others. Performance practice
certainly improves language use and comprehension, but it is not
a precondition for either the understanding of meaning or the
formulation of content. Understanding a verbal language consists
primarily of understanding its syntax, though not necessarily
replicating it; it is a discovery of the *process* by which content
is formulated, of the speaker's intention to mean. In music,
satisfaction may be derived without absolute agreement about
the meaning of the code; that is, the creator's intention to mean
can be offset by a performer's or listener's intention to make
sense, without any of the absence of communication that would
occur if a listener misunderstood a speaker's intention to mean.

In music, it is not essential for listeners or performers to
understand the creator's intended syntax or even the intended
meaning, as long as they can find *a* syntax and their own meanings in the music. Although modern research has challenged
much 'traditional' performance practice, it is very *un*likely that
even the most 'authentic', carefully researched performances of
Baroque music will be able to convey to twentieth-century
audiences the intentions of the composers or the musical experience of seventeenth- or eighteenth-century listeners, because our
ears are differently tuned, and we cannot recreate the same sonic
environment. The sounds of Beethoven's Fifth Symphony can
never again be startling and new in the same way that they were
to Goethe and his contemporaries. When people hear them even
for the first time in the 1980s, they listen with ears that have
almost certainly heard Brahms, Wagner, Stravinsky, jazz, or pop,
and the sonic impact of the music is bound to be different.

Information about the social and cultural background of new
sounds can often be a hindrance to enjoying and assimilating
them, and I rarely read programme notes until after a performance. The music of Schubert and Mozart has always appealed to
me not as specimens of Austrian culture, but as beautiful music.
Of course music is embedded in the particular conventions of
composers' environments and historical periods, but the whole

point of understanding music *as music* is that we carry the cognitive equipment to transcend cultural boundaries and resonate at the common level of humanity. As Constant Lambert said at the end of *Music Ho*!

> The artist who is one of a group writes for that group alone, whereas the artist who expresses personal experience may in the end reach universal experience.   (Lambert 1966:280)

Information about the circumstances of musical composition and the cultural environment of a composer can explain details of technique and style that had currency at the time of conception of a work, and especially the significance of the nonverbal signs that were used. But these are the external products of processes of musical thought that were constructed in particular social situations. For people who were *not* involved in those particular situations, their meanings coincide as far as they can make sense of the music in terms of their own experience. Inevitably, this can be done only by invoking different cultural conventions that are familiar to listeners or performers, or by resonance with universal structures of the human mind that were used in the act of musical creation.

Thus all the cultural information about Venda and other African musics, on which my work as an ethnomusicologist has been based, was in a sense extraneous to my understanding of the music as music. Even if I knew exactly how the Venda conceived and perceived their music, I could not possibly experience it in the same way as them, because of different habits of processing experience. Moreover, as I pointed out in the second chapter, there were several different patterns of interpretation amongst the Venda themselves. It is, in fact, as ridiculous to say that knowledge of a culture is necessary for appreciation of music that has been created by people reared in it, as it is to say that music helps us to understand the culture of the people who created it. What music tells us about the culture of the music-makers can only be known when we have studied their culture. Schubert's and Mahler's music tells me nothing about Austrian and Viennese culture until I find out about those cultures and try to make connections between this knowledge and my experience of the music. Similarly, if I want to understand and appreciate *music*, my best course is to get on with listening to it and performing it – provided, of course, that the sociological conditions I outlined in the last chapter have been fulfilled. This is a matter of using as far as possible the nonverbal cognitive apparatus that I have as a human being, rather than the particular forms of it that have been emphasized in my own society.

It is interesting that many people sight-read a piece of music far better than they play it for the second and third time. I have also found that I can learn to play a piece to the satisfaction of a critical audience by trusting my musical intuition rather than examining its technique. I find formal analysis less helpful than listening to alternative performances of the same or similar works and hearing my own repeated performances, in which I explore different ways of feeling the music physically and technically – whether it be discovering alternative fingerings and arm movements at the keyboard or alternative ways of conducting a passage.

I found that the same principles of understanding have applied to my learning of African musics, though it took a lot of listening and watching to get used to the different idioms. I learnt to perform first and asked questions afterwards – not so much because I thought it would help me to understand the music better, but because I was interested to know why I liked it, or why people said it was the same as something that didn't sound the same to me. I learnt most from the experience of performance practice, especially when my performance was considered wrong.

This raises the problem of how much *physical* performance is actually necessary for understanding music. I have argued that performance is a way of knowing, and that listening is as much performance as actually singing and playing. In fact, performance can sometimes interfere with attentive listening, as any pianist knows very well. It is quite possible to play efficiently without hearing what you play. I have also insisted that one goal of musical progress must be to abolish the division between mental and manual labour in the arts. There cannot be any hard and fast rule about the relative merits of performing privately with gramophone records, going to a concert hall and participating in someone else's live performance, or actually performing with a group or on one's own. My experiences in Africa in learning to understand alien musical traditions have convinced me that at least some experience of physical performance is necessary in order to understand certain principles of music-making, and especially the relationships between body movement and musical ideas, which I discussed in chapters 3, 4 and 5.

On the other hand, there are occasions when participation in performance can be counter-productive. For example, while I was staying in Perth, Western Australia, I attended the openings of two exhibitions of aboriginal art at which groups of musicians performed. At the Perth Art Gallery, a speaker introduced the music and asked us to join him in saying some aboriginal words. Then the musicians began to perform, but they were constantly interrupted by explanations, translations, and requests to the audience to say aboriginal words, clap, sit down in aboriginal fashion, and so on. The result was that we never heard more than a few seconds of music at a time and most of it was drowned by our own clapping.

At the opening of an exhibition of the Nexus gallery in Fremantle, on the other hand, the musicians and dancers were allowed to perform without any interruptions. We all became involved in the movement and the music, without necessarily knowing anything about their cultural significance. Above all, we could observe the transformations in the faces and bodies of the performers as the music progressed and the performance became more intense. The man who led the group corroboree became radiant, though slightly puffed with the effort, and he did not have to do more than announce that they were enjoying themselves so much that they could dance another corroboree. I think we all understood and appreciated the music and dance because of the power of the performance, the display of technique and the transformation of the performers. Had we been asked to participate with our own untutored movements, we might have missed the subtleties of difference between men's and women's movements, and the skilful flow of the music and dance. And had the performance been interrupted with explanation, we could not have tuned in with our nonverbal receptors to what was timeless, placeless, and truly artistic about the aboriginal music and dance.

I have enthused about recorded performances of music because they are the ultimate in musical detachment for the listener. They allow intimate, personal experiences of music, private performances if you like, in which people are free to move around, laugh, weep and express every range of emotion that the music inspires in them. Recorded performances have also had profound effects on the shape of world musics and have been used as models for new and exciting compositions.

Musical structures both evoke and spring from 'feelings', and especially the feelings associated with internal body movements. Human feelings are also structured; and in the transformation of feelings into patterns of sound and vice versa, the structures of the body play a part in creation and interpretation, no less than the musical conventions of different societies and the different musical experiences of individuals.

It is sometimes said that an Englishman cannot possibly understand African, Indian, and other non-English musics. This seems to me as wrong-headed as the view of many white settlers in Africa, who claimed that blacks could not possibly appreciate and perform properly Handel's *Messiah*, English part-songs, or Lutheran hymns. Of course music is not a universal language, and musical traditions are probably the most esoteric of all cultural products. But the experience of ethnomusicologists, and the growing popularity of non-European musics in Europe and America and of 'Western' music in the Third World, suggest that the cultural barriers are somewhat illusory, externally imposed, and concerned more with verbal rationalizations and explanations of music and its association with specific social events, than with the music itself. The flexibility and adaptability of music as a symbol system are such that there are as many variations of interpretation and understanding *amongst* Englishmen, Africans and Indians, as there are between them. Different musical systems often coincide with cultural boundaries, and subdivisions of musical style, musical activities and experiences are labelled and discussed with the general language of a culture. But a shared mode of discourse does not provide members of different classes, families and occupational groups with common feelings and mutual understanding any more than French culture gives all French people the same personality.

Because music is concerned with feelings which are primarily individual and rooted in the body, its structural and sensuous elements resonate more with individuals' cognitive and emotional sets than with their cultural sentiments, although its external manner and expression are rooted in historical circumstances. This is why the English could still enjoy Beethoven when at war with the Germans, and why it often makes more sense to relate the output of a composer to music from another society or to someone from the past, than to his/her immediate musical neighbour.

When the words and labels of a cultural tradition are put aside and 'form in tonal motion' is allowed to speak for itself, there is a good chance that English, Africans, and Indians will experience similar feelings, especially if they perform the music. Because their bodies have a common repertory of somatic states and cognitive functions, musical symbols can be inherently effective and enable their users to share transcendence of time, place and culture. They are effective as symbols because their production involves bodies in similar patterns of movements in space and time, with corresponding physiological responses, so that their inherent meaning is, as it were, forced upon performers by the very process of doing them.

Performance is the essence of the musical event, but although it makes aesthetic experience possible it does not guarantee it. First, the production of musical symbols is only one of several interrelated channels of communication that must be involved; secondly, listening to music is as important in appreciation as playing it, and a non-playing listener can sometimes hear and feel more clearly than a player. 'Artistic' activities can be performed as a routine, like driving a car to work, and in such cases I doubt if they should be called 'artistic' or 'aesthetic', even if they do involve music-making, painting, or sculpture. At the same time, there are some corporate activities, like music-making, which by their formal structure and stated intent are more likely than not to generate aesthetic experience.

To define aesthetic experience in terms of particular kinds of products called 'the arts', rather than special humanizing processes in which organisms communicate with self, other and environment, is to pay lip-service to bourgeois definitions and uses of art and to restrict the creativity and emotional expression of mankind. But to recognize that some kinds of communication are generally more effective than others at stimulating love, co-operation and gentleness, developing and refining the senses and educating the emotions, is to acknowledge that social and cultural organization is far from perfect, and that most people are not yet sufficiently advanced to be able to do everything in a state of transcendental awareness.

MUSICAL PERFORMANCE AND CULTURAL HEGEMONY

Percy Grainger was deeply concerned about performances of music which many people could enjoy, and about the extension of music education to cover the whole world's music. These aims cannot be achieved without changes in the contexts and uses of music, and in people's attitudes to it. In the last chapter I argued that the power of music depends on how it is defined and used in social and intellectual life, as much as on its musical structure. The first step on the road of musical progress is therefore political and communal: musical life must be re-organized so that the power of music can be used and not abused. The ultimate goal is personal and social transformation: music-making must be used to enhance personal consciousness and experience in community. The proper study of music is music-making, just as the proper study of religion is worship, and not dogma. As Percy Grainger claimed on many occasions, the most politically effective use of music in society is the harnessing of aesthetic energy so that all individuals can obtain full ownership of their senses.

Cultural politics, the use of culture and the arts to promote political interests, invariably exploits and contains the power of music, as Maurice Bloch implied in his analysis of the use of song and dance to restrict political argument. It diverts attention from the real political issues or simply asserts the hegemony of its promoters. But at our present stage in the world history of music and music-making, we cannot get down to the true business of studying and experiencing music as music without confronting the politics of culture as a major issue. Music-making, like relgious worship, has become so bogged down in abuses, irrelevancies, false trails, elitisms, and misconceptions, that we shall have to do a lot of political work to restore it to its rightful place in modern societies. We have to gain acceptance even for the simple facts that all normal human beings have the capacities for making music; that music is discovered as well as invented; that music is essentially a primary modelling system, and not only an epiphenomenon of something else; that unwritten music can be as complex as written music, because of the universal complexity of the human mind, and so on.

In 1915, Percy Grainger made the most original and revolutionary proposition that 'a world-wide International Musical Society' should be formed 'for the purpose of making all the world's music known to all the world by means of imported performances, phonograph and gramophone records and adequate notations' (Balough 1982:78).

The International Music Council, the International Folk Music Council (now the International Council for Traditional Music), and the Society for Ethnomusicology were formed in the 1940s and 1950s; in the 1950s and 1960s, Mantle Hood and David McAllester in the USA pioneered the performance of Asian and African musics as an integral part of the training of university students in music and ethnomusicology; Indonesian music has been taught in Australian universities and in the Netherlands, and Indian music in Dartington College of Arts, Devon; European music has been taught side by side with traditional music in, for example, China, India, Korea, Japan, Kenya, Ghana, Nigeria, Uganda, and Zambia; and in the 1970s some British universities began to develop ethnomusicology programmes and encourage performance. But we are still a very long way from realizing Grainger's far-sighted vision, especially in the well-established colleges and academies of music. I can think of several places where an imaginative student would be greeted with much the same retort as the boy Percy Grainger when he asked the Frankfurt teacher who wanted him to enter for the Mendelssohn Prize for piano playing,

> 'If I should win, would they let me study Chinese music in China with the money?'
> The teacher replied:
> 'No, they don't give prizes to idiots.'   (Balough 1982:78)

Percy Grainger returned to this theme again and again, and in the 1934 lectures he stressed two very important points: He insisted that music is *not* a universal language, and that its message is essentially personal.

Grainger called his first 1934 lecture 'The Universalist Attitude toward Music':

We are continually hearing that 'music is a universal language', yet the facts prove that music, as practised and enjoyed to-day, is the most parochial and least universal of the arts...We are quite needlessly ignorant of folk-music, primitive music, and the great art-musics of Asia.

What would we think of a Professor of Literature who knew nothing of Homer, the Icelandic sagas, the Japanese Heiki Monogatori, Chaucer, Dante and Edgar Lee Masters? We would think him a joke. Yet we see nothing strange in a Professor of Music who knows nothing of primitive music and folk-music, the music of mediaeval Europe, and the great art-musics of Asia, and who knows next to nothing of contemporary music.

It seems to me that the commonsense view of music is to approach all the world's available music with an open mind, just as we approach the world's literature or painting or philosophy. It seems to me that we should be willing, even eager, to hear everything we can of all kinds of music, from whatever quarter and whatever era, in order that *we may find out from experience whether or not it carries any spiritual message for us as individuals.* (Appendix A:151–2; italics mine)

Grainger's general philosophy and specific proposals were concerned with the politics of music, rather than the political uses of music. He wanted 'subscription concerts...in the art-centres of all lands' (Balough 1982:78) and performance and listening as part of the serious business of music education. He wanted people to listen critically to all kinds of music and to respect their variety and originality as products of the complexity of the human mind and of cultural traditions. He did not ask everyone to appreciate and enjoy all that they heard, as musical taste is a very personal matter. Even ethnomusicologists are not required to enjoy as well as understand the many different musical styles that they study, and there need be no embarrassment about liking some cultural products of a society more than others. I tend to prefer English painting, music, and gardens to English food. If I prefer Ugandan to Tanzanian musics, I am not expressing preferences for the cultures and societies in which their musics are embedded, and certainly not a preference for their political systems, either before or after the depositions of the Kabaka and Idi Amin.

And yet a great deal of our appreciation of world music confuses cultural chauvinism with musical taste. Performances of traditional music are too often associated with cultural bunfights, folklore festivals, and political jamborees in which various exotic musics, dances and associated arts are dished up for the promotion of national or ethnic causes. Many people's experiences of other worlds of music are derived entirely from such contexts, and there are two serious disadvantages. First, the music that is presented is often not truly representative of the tradition that is advertised; and secondly, because of the context, the aims of musical exchange and mutual understanding are defeated.

The terms 'folk' dance and 'folk' music are products of bourgeois ideology, which arose from a particular European form of the capitalist mode of production: the cultures and ethnic identity of communities of peasant producers had been besieged by the exploitation of labour and the mass exodus from the rural areas to new industrial centres. As the power of the urban proletariat grew, so did the nostalgia of the bourgeoisie for the disappearing countryside and ways of country people. It was in this context that the science of folklore was born, and it is necessary to be aware of the dangers and contradictions inherent in its bourgeois conceptual framework. For many decades, and even today in some countries, the science of folklore concerned itself with rural customs and largely ignored the new folklore of the urban proletariat, which in England has been studied by scholars like A. L. Lloyd (1967), and more recently by members of the Centre for Cultural Studies at the University of Birmingham.

The presentation and propagation of folklore can be politically oppressive or politically uplifting. But it can never be *non*-political, and the performances of so-called 'national' teams do not necessarily represent national culture or the interests of more than small sections of their populations. For instance, the performance of the group that officially represented England in 1978 at the International Folklore Festival in Bourgas, Bulgaria, did not depict or reflect the 'folk' life of the people of London, let alone the English nation. There was no trace of the lives of black British populations or of the new counter-culture that Meredith Tax (1972) described in her article: 'Culture Is Not Neutral, Whom Does It Serve?'

Folk festivals and multinational cultural events tend *not* to breed in different groups respect for each other's music and dances, and people often equate the most attractive displays with some kind of general cultural superiority. Poles, Hungarians,

English, Irish, Chinese and Indians go away more convinced than ever that their own products are superior to others' and that they have little or nothing to learn. The atmosphere is rather like that of the Olympic Games, where nations take credit for the performance of individuals. The political claptrap diverts people's attention from the only possible *musical* experiences that are to be gained from such performances, the experiences of nonverbal communication which help to *transcend* cultural boundaries.

THE POPULAR PRESENTATION OF MUSIC AS PART OF SOCIAL LIFE

Meredith Tax described a different type of collective effort which is closer to the kinds of situation that Percy Grainger envisaged and that I encountered in Africa. The integration of different media and the emphasis on the experience of performance, rather than its political uses, tend to arouse people's aesthetic sensibilities more than the folklore festival performances. Three important changes were discerned in the new British counter-culture:

The first is that this culture is in many cases the product of collective efforts rather than of bourgeois individualism. Rock groups, street theatre groups, poster workshops, art crews for demonstrations – all of these are forms of creativity that are social and shared.

The second thing is that many of these cultural forms are conceived of as participatory; these would include a lot of theatre which demands audience participation and response; poetry which demands being read out loud; and music that needs dance to fulfil it, and which is participated in by people who dance.

The third thing is that many of these new art expressions mix media and genres to a new extent. The rock groups that combine posters, slides, light shows, music, poetry, dance and special effects are one example. Such art breaks down very old divisions of labour; and any breakdown of the division of labour in the arts seems a hopeful sign of our growing ability to integrate different kinds of experience. (Tax 1972:26–7)

Thus art and life are reconciled, and the mixing of media and their associated symbols provides a large number of people with the opportunity of *working together*. Situations such as these can produce a deep sense of personal satisfaction and group solidarity, and provide opportunities both for the creation of new artistic forms and for the popular presentation and performance of different musical traditions as part of social life.

Inevitably, traditional forms will be performed out of their original contexts, as the Hawai'ian *hula* has become re-interpreted to suit modern needs. They can be presented effectively as non-verbal communication, without verbiage about their socio-cultural context and extra-musical significance. Moreover, concert halls and formal stages may not be the best environments for the presentation of 'folk' and 'traditional' musics, and the more varied community contexts may be as appropriate for this as they are for the invention of new music. Use of open spaces and natural environments provide opportunities for composers to explore new sonorities, new ensembles, and new combinations of art forms.

It is surprising that Australian artistic life seems still to be a little constricted by the European traditions of enclosed concert halls, theatres and galleries, which were a result of Europe's climate, the structure of its social and political life and its patterns of urban development, and its use of the arts as entertainments for leisure time rather than as integral parts of the business of living. The York Festival in Western Australia is a fine example of a break with this tradition, and its ultimate success will depend on the extent to which it becomes part of the communal life of the people of York, rather than an annual invasion of York. This has, of course, been one of the problems faced by the organizers of festivals and community arts enterprises in the United Kingdom and United States of America. If it is successfully solved, much will have been done to restore music to its former place as a truly popular activity.

'Festivals' were an integral part of popular life in many parts of Africa, and I think this is why many Africans have been unhappy about the formal presentation of folklore, as in FESTAC, the Second World Black and African Festival of Arts and Culture. First, the concepts of 'folk' music, 'folk' dance, and 'folklore' are irrelevant and even politically objectionable to many people in Sub-Saharan Africa. There is music, dance, and all the associated arts that are part of a *living* tradition shared by the whole community.

Secondly, African music and dance have traditionally depended very much on the creative interaction of performers and audience, and on a high degree of intimacy and mutual understanding. At the distance required for many formal presentations,

you cannot see or hear the variations that make every performance a unique experience. However, the meanings of 'folk' dance
and music must inevitably change as soon as they are presented.
It is a new context and it brings with it a new set of meanings.

Such contrasts of presentation and of meaning were not absent
in rural contexts. In a study of *bepha* (Blacking 1962), the Venda
name for a musical expedition, I described an institution that is
similar to the exchange of folklore teams undertaken by members
of the International Council of Organizers of Folk Festivals
(CIOFF). For over two months, a girls' dance team had daily
rehearsals, which led up to a four-day visit to another district.
There were differences between the social relations and performance in rehearsals and in the public display. One interesting
feature was that although members of the visiting and hosting
dance teams spoke the same language, the dance exchange did
not lead to closer relationships between them. Rather, it consolidated relationships *among* members of the same team, who
belonged to one political unit, and *between* the officials and
managers of the teams, who were interested as much in the
political relationships between the two areas as in the dance and
music themselves. Much the same pattern of relations existed
between members of teams and team organizers at the Bourgas
festival.

In the African exchange, the authenticity and intimacy of the
tradition was maintained. The four-day spectacle was itself part
of tradition, just as folklore festivals and exchanges are becoming
a part of the traditions of industrial societies. The exchange was
an important focus of activity, but what happened during the
previous two months' rehearsals and afterwards was really more
important. The way things were done during the four-day spectacle emphasized the political nature of the dance and music —
'political', that is, in the sense of promoting harmonious and
productive human interaction. Audiences participated, and some
even shared the labour of drumming and dancing. They were
close enough to interact with the performers, rather than merely
react to them. The intimate nuances of the dance, music, and
costumes could be meaningful in ways that might have been lost
in purely staged presentations.

I found that in African dance and music in general, events were
skilfully transformed from occasions for strident display to

occasions for subtlety and intimacy, from experiences of society and community to experiences of individuality, and vice versa. The gentleness and intimacy of much 'folk' music are too often forgotten in the hearty atmosphere that pervades some 'folk'-festivals and public presentations of folklore.

Intimacy is, of course, generally absent from symphony concerts and mammoth presentations of works like Bach's *St John Passion*, which were designed for entirely different environments; though it can be obtained by subtle treatment of parts of the orchestra, as in Mahler's symphonies. It can also be obtained by personal involvement in performance and recognition of the fact that the power of music comes to us through the sense that we make of it.

WORLD MUSICS IN SCHOOLS

Percy Grainger's arguments for the performance of world music were not addressed specifically to problems of music education. But he expressed views which were like those of Zoltán Kodály. He felt that 'the basis of all art is racial', 'and that the way of great creative art is from the local to the national to the universal' (Balough 1982A:92).

It is the infusion of deep personality and broad erudition into the task of voicing national and racial traits that entitles men such as Grieg, Chopin, Tchaikovsky, Delius, and Albeniz to the title of first-class geniuses [1920].

... this kind of patriotism is free of all chauvinism, defeats nobody and enriches the rest of the world while it enriches us.

... the patriotism that finds its vent in racial self-expression through the medium of art does not wilt and die as empires and supremacies wilt and die, but lives on through the ages, a 'carte de visite' to future humanity, engendering cosmic love [1919].   (Balough 1982A:92)

Helen Reeves commented on these views in relation to Grainger's 'universalist outlook':

Music as a universal language is not an end in itself, but is seen as a vehicle for world peace and the unification of mankind. This should not be interpreted as music being a *cosmopolitan* expression of mankind-as-a-whole. Grainger says that, as a musician, he always tried to play all the world's music because he saw 'in Negro music the spirit of the

Negro race, in Jewish music the spirit of the Jewish race, in Anglo-Saxon music the spirit of the Anglo-Saxon race, and so on'. So whilst he sees all music as moving gradually towards the same goal, he nevertheless recognizes music as separate strands of artistic expression by people of many different cultures or, as Grainger calls these separate musical strands, 'the threads of unity'. (Reeves 1982:47)

Kodály's arguments about the local and national roots of musical expression were similar, though they were motivated by different experiences and tied to a theory for the reform of music education in Hungary. In a lecture on Hungarian music education, given in 1945, he argued that:

it is the works expressing most strongly the artist's own national characteristics which have the greatest world-wide apeal...individual originality can be rooted only in a national originality.

(Kodály 1974:152)

The road from Hungarian music to the understanding of international music is easy, but in the opposite direction the road is difficult, or non-existent.

Thus we need a Hungarian musical education, both from a Hungarian and from an international point of view. The more Hungarian we are the more can we expect an international interest. And this is the only way in which we can achieve a Hungarian musical culture.

(Kodály 1974:154)

Kodály specified what he meant by 'a Hungarian musical culture'. He lamented that his country was musically divided into those who were musically educated in a foreign tradition, without any feeling for Hungarian character, and those who felt Hungarian music to be their very own but were 'musically absolutely uneducated' and 'therefore, unable to comprehend a more demanding composition' (Kodály 1974:153). He advocated a programme of training in Hungarian folk music from the earliest kindergarten stage, and concluded; 'At this point democracy means two things: one is to make the means of musical education available to everybody, and the other a full assertion of national characteristics' (Kodály 1974:155).

Grainger's and Kodály's emphasis on national character in music creates problems, particularly when it is used to justify the kinds of excess that I discussed earlier in this chapter. Kodály's remarks, in particular, can be misinterpreted as narrow chauvinism if it is forgotten that at the time of writing he was

passionately concerned with the freedom and intellectual inde-
pendence of the Hungarian people from foreign hegemony:

Shall we continue to be a colony or shall we become an independent
country, not only politically but culturally, in asserting our own
personality, too?   (Kodály 1974:154)

Until very recently the training of professional musicians was in the
hands of foreigners who did not know Hungarian and lived here as
aristocratic foreigners.   (*ibid.*)

Kodály supported his political views with theories of music
education which cannot be sustained: there is no convincing
evidence that 'a multilingual child will not know any language
well' (think of George Steiner, for instance!); that 'a child
nurtured on mixed music will not feel musically at home any-
where' (there are thousands of African and Asian children who
are quite happy in their bimusicality); or that 'if we do not want
to rear children as aliens, we can do nothing else but teach these
tunes' (i.e. a collection of Hungarian songs) (Kodály 1974:153).
These kinds of argument deny that the crucial factor in all
musical experience is how people make sense of what they define
as music, and that young people have the innate capacity to
discriminate and make their own choices. As I have already
pointed out in earlier chapters, culture does not determine
people's behaviour in some mysterious way, and musical systems
are only cultural conventions which individuals can use as
frameworks for musical communication.

Kodály's enthusiasm for the social and moral consequences
of choral singing also led him to a curious conclusion: 'We must
lead great masses to music. An instrumental culture can never
become a culture of masses. Instruments have become expensive
and the number of pupils learning to play instruments has fallen'
(Kodály 1974:123). During the past fifty years, ethnomusicological research has shown that an instrumental culture *can*
become a culture of the masses even when instruments are
expensive and take much time and care to manufacture: the
polyphony of African ensembles and the heterophony of Balinese
gamelan are examples of popular styles of music-making which
fulfil the criteria that Kodály found in choral singing.

Some of Kodály's statements about the precise effects of music
also need revision in the light of ethnomusicological research,

although the basic principles of his argument are sound. For example, he wrote in 1941:

Taken separately, too, the elements of music are precious instruments in education. Rhythm develops attention, concentration, determination and the ability to condition oneself. Melody opens up the world of emotions. Dynamic variation and tone colour sharpen our hearing. Singing, finally, is such a many-sided physical activity that its effect in physical education is immeasurable – if there is perhaps anyone to whom the education of the spirit does not matter. Its beneficial effect in health is well known; special books have been written on this.

(Kodály 1974:130)

The point is that the elements of music have different significance in different cultural contexts: 'rhythm', 'melody', 'tonality', 'harmony' etc. cannot be treated cognitively and emotionally as absolute categories. In any case, they cannot in themselves have effects on people; and so the important point is how people make sense of the different elements of music that *they* identify. The case of African drumming illustrates this well: most people trained in a European musical tradition tend to emphasize its rhythmic characteristics or the 'messages' that the drums can transmit (thus confusing the uses of drums as music, as poetry, and as a sort of Morse Code). Anyone who spends time in Africa and learns from African musicians will soon find that drums are invariably perceived as *melodic* instruments, and 'polyrhythms' as poly*phony*. These are important musical conventions that must be understood if performances of African music are to have value in music education. It is possible for United Kingdom citizens of Caribbean and African origin to hear and interpret African music in an *un*African way, as indeed many Western-educated Africans have misunderstood the traditional music of their own countries. I have attended classes and performances of African music in the United Kingdom where the subtleties and gentle beauty of the music are suppressed by an emphasis on noise and rhythm and a Boy-Scout-camp attitude to performance. African music is often popular, in the sense that everyone in the community appreciates it and most people like to participate in performance; but the ethos of much African traditional music is 'classical', and it should be treated with the same 'seriousness' as the music of Bach and Mozart and Beethoven.

Kodály was well aware of similar problems in the use of

Hungarian music. In examining the role of music in 'educating the nation', he insisted that he did 'not mean some stupid irredentist songs, complete with banner-waving, dressed up in sham-Hungarian mummery' (Kodály 1974:130). In his critique of particular songs and methods in the building of Hungarian character, he emphasised how much children can learn in kindergarten (54 songs in 18 months! – Kodály 1974:139), and in discussing song texts, he emphasized that 'the child delights in the play of musical forms at a stage when he does not care about the meaning of the text' (Kodály 1974:142). I found this to be true of the music-making of Venda children (Blacking 1967:30), and it reminds us that we can enjoy music from different parts of the world without having long lectures about the cultural background. That can come later, when childen have been allowed to use their 'direct intuition'. 'Often a single experience will open the young soul to music for a whole lifetime. This experience cannot be left to chance, it is the duty of the school to provide it' (Kodály 1974:120). And because of the familiarity of musical sounds *that are not treated as music*, children's *musical* enlightenment may well come from encounters with the unfamiliar: from Balinese gamelan rather than British popular song, from the *Kora* playing of Amadu Jobarteh[18] rather than the singing of Shirley Bassey, and from music for the sitar rather than the electric guitar.

Kodály emphasized that young people are capable of the greatest achievements in musical skill if given the chance, and that adult music will take care of itself if children have good singing teachers (Kodály 1974:124). He also complained about the futility of producing a host of professional musicians from the musical academies without any consumers at home (Kodály 1974:127): they had to find work abroad, and the nation gained nothing from their export. 'Audiences for whom high-level music is a necessity must be reared' (Kodály 1974:125). Thus, as for so many social and economic problems in industrial countries, the solution is to be found not primarily in commercial enterprises, or in money and technology per se, but in education and the expansion of educational opportunities – not for the strictly vocational purposes of getting a living, but for living a full and creative life. Arts Council subsidies would hardly be necessary if music education were 'successful', and a case could be made for diverting all Arts Council funds for secondary, tertiary and continuing arts education.

As I contemplate the divided society in which I live, I find it curious to read of Kodály comparing the social solidarity of British society favourably with the lack of it in Hungary. He suggested that this could be due to the discipline of singing in choirs. He later argued (in 1941!) that 'Germany's great musical culture would never have reached its present level without the teaching of singing having been systematically carried out in schools for centuries' (Kodály 1974:128). He rejected the idea that the economic crisis was the cause of everything in 1929:

Everything will be set right as soon as the economy is in order? I do not think so. Penury may hamper development, but wealth does not promote it either. Money does not produce ideas . . . The recent development of music in Hungary is a straight refutation of the economic view of history.
(Kodály 1974:126)

Kodály shared most of Grainger's views on music education, and he expressed them more systematically, so that they have influenced music education in Hungary and many other parts of the world. Kodály saw music education as central to the general education of the young – provided that it really was a progressive, expansive, demanding system of *musical* education and not a sub-species of community action. The communal aspects of music-making were important not so much because they confirmed and consolidated the identity of groups, but because they enhanced the consciousness of individuals and cultivated 'their talent to the highest degree' (Kodály 1974:199).

By 'community education', and 'adjustment to the human community', which 'not even the most careful education in the family can supply' (Kodály 1974:129), Kodály meant much more than a mere togetherness and common sense of purpose. The role of music 'in educating the nation' was to be achieved by dedicated, self-conscious performance practice, which cultivated the potential of individual and social bodies.

If we take the general principles of Kodály's system and detach them from the specific historical contexts in which he thought and wrote about Hungarian nationalism; if we treat Grainger's 'racial' and 'cultural' theories of musical expression as ways of talking about the influences of environment and enculturation on the musical *conventions* which people choose; if we treat cultures as floating resources, available for use, rather than as determinants of human thought and behaviour; if we recall what both composers wrote about the importance of individuality in music and of *individual* musical experience (cf. Appendix A: 151–2, quoted on p. 133 above), it becomes clear that they were not advocating the kind of policies that are sometimes promoted as 'multicultural' education, which reached their ultimate absurdity in the South African system of different education systems and syllabuses for separated racial and cultural groups.

They were concerned with education in and through music that is closely related to the local community and natural environment. Because of their different notions of community and environment, Kodály wanted this music to be basically Hungarian, while Grainger wanted it to be world music. Grainger's upbringing in Australia, without experience of the conflicts and narrow rivalries of Europe, probably inspired his more expansive solution, which is particularly suitable for music education in countries with substantial numbers of citizens who are the descendants of first or second generation immigrants. The United Kingdom is a case in point where Percy Grainger's solution can be applied.

A *British* music education, rooted in English, Scottish, Welsh, and Irish folk song is no longer appropriate for a nation whose citizens have comparatively recent ties to India, Pakistan, Hong Kong, Cyprus, Poland, and the Caribbean. It would not be musically beneficial, even in the light of Kodály's theories, to bring up the children of immigrants specifically with the music of their ancestors, since that music does not really belong to the local community and natural environment. Oppressed and minority groups may find it necessary to emphasize their cultural heritage as part of political and educational campaigns to improve their condition; but responses to such movements by state patronage of 'multicultural' education only serve to deny the essentially monocultural nature of the state and its education system and to reinforce cultural stereotypes. The music of immigrant communities thereby becomes 'ethnic' music, a spurious category which insults the creators of the music and ignores the fact that Indian music, African music, Balinese music etc. are, like European music, created not by some amorphous collective, but by individual composers and performers, who are known and recognized in their communities as were Bach in Leipzig, Beethoven in Bonn, and Schubert in Vienna. People and artistic traditions have been reclassified in curious ways: learning 'African' music has come to mean learning one or two genres of Ghanaian music; and although the term 'Afro-Caribbean' underlines the common experience of colonialism and may be useful for political activism in the United Kingdom, it effectively denies the uniqueness and inventiveness of Caribbean societies and the diversity and ancient history of African societies.

Similarly, the concept of a 'multicultural' society tends to focus, implicitly and often explicitly, on the life-styles of Asian, Caribbean, Cypriot, and other 'exotic' peoples in the United Kingdom. Thus it tends to ignore the deeply rooted differences in the cultures of natives of the United Kingdom whose families have lived in the country for generations.

There are, for instance, significant differences between the life-styles and values of people who live in the north, south-west and south-east of England; between social classes; between art worlds, business worlds, agricultural worlds and bureaucratic worlds; and between fundamentally different types of Christian denomination. If cultural differences exist at all, they can be used to separate very similar social groups, no matter how trivial they may be. And conversely, the existence of considerable cultural differences in two social groups need not prevent them from becoming closely related. The effects of cultural differences on social action depend on how people perceive and use them. The cultural differences between English-speaking Christians whose families have lived in England for at least eight generations can be as great as the differences between English-speaking families and immigrant families of Gujerati-speaking Hindus or Urdu-speaking Moslems. If the differences between different English people are minimized and those between English and others are emphasized, it is partly because it is politically expedient to do so, and partly because differences in racial type, language, and religion are more easily marked. But race and language are not necessarily coterminous with culture, and religion is only one aspect of a cultural system. Moreover, the divisions within another faith such as Islam, which may appear monolithic to many English Christians, are as great as the divisions within Christianity.

If there is such a phenomenon as a British national character, there is a sense in which it has been 'multicultural' for at least 200 years. It has been deeply affected by the colonial experience. The 'British' national drink is tea – from India or China. Many British men and women wear pyjamas at night, an idea from China. They consume vast quantities of sugar originally from Jamaica and the Caribbean, and cocoa, primarily from West Africa. They also drink a great deal of coffee, from Kenya. I need hardly say how diet has been enriched by Chinese and Indian food, and how many characteristically British dishes are colonial in origin, such as the kedgeree that we had at my school, and the rice pudding. The English language is full of words of Asian and African origin. British domestic furniture has been profoundly influenced by Asian styles and practice. Even an interest in Eastern religions is the result *not* of immigration, but often of British citizens coming home after a period of foreign service in the army, the civil service, or some firm.

Music is essentially about aesthetic experiences and the creative expression of individual human beings in community, about the sharing of feelings and ideas. Many musicians have composed for their loved ones, their own friends, and their own musical groups or religious congregations. They were not greatly concerned with nations or ethnic groups, except when they were exiled or when national themes and interests were fashionable; artificial boundaries are inimical to the spirit of art and human brotherhood. The purpose of music education, as Kodály frequently emphasized, should be to help individuals to develop their aesthetic experience and understanding by exercising their powers of discrimination.

Schools provide the opportunity for music-making to take place in new contexts, and for pupils to make sense of both familiar and unfamiliar music in new ways. This in itself can enhance the aesthetic appreciation by diminishing obvious social applications, and so allow young people to delight 'in the play of musical forms', as Kodály suggested (Kodály 1974: 142).

How those musical forms are presented is no less important than what music is offered. In expanding the range of British music education, it is not just a question of What can we bring in from India or the Caribbean? but How can we combat narrow-mindedness, racism, prejudice in school books, and ethno-centricism in education? How can we teach people through music-making that there is a larger social world outside and a richer world of experience inside each individual? If British music education is to reflect a multicultural society, its task is not so much to make blacks feel at home in school, as to make sure that white children are really aware of the historical and cultural traditions of their black neighbours. In order to counteract ethnocentric and derogatory classifications of music (e.g. Bach, Beethoven, Mozart, Debussy, Duke Ellington etc. versus 'ethnic' music), emphasis must be laid on the contributions of individual composers and performers.[19] Education authorities must ensure that schools have visits and workshops by highly skilled per-formers of compositions and genres that have been developed in Asia and Africa, as well as by pianists and violinists. It is necessary for children to hear a piano recital by a Jamaican or an Indian and a sitar recital by an English person, if only to demon-strate the individuality and transcendental universality of the arts.

The aim of music in schools must not be to reinforce tribal boundaries or to encourage tokenism by concentrating on pop music in predominantly 'working-class' schools, reggae in schools with children of Caribbean origin, or Urdu folk-songs where there are majorities of Pakistanis. It is not the business of music educators to subvent community activities, which already exist, or to encourage cultural brokers to mobilize new social groups for social, political or religious purposes. Music education should not be used to emphasize culture, because as soon as that happens there arise arguments about cultural hegemony, as well as false notions of what culture is: it should emphasize *human* variety and ingenuity. Music education should not be cosy or comfortable; for music as passive entertainment, or as sensuous gratification of totemic identities, is invariably corrupting. It is the business of music educators to induce in all their pupils new *artistic* experiences, which may or may not generate new social experiences.

Educators in the United Kingdom have a responsibility to transmit the fruits of one of the Great Traditions, a civilization that followed on from those of Africa and Asia and Latin America and happens to be influential in the world at the moment. This tradition cannot be associated only with social groups of European origin, because it is an amalgam of the inventions and ideas of individuals from Egypt, Iraq, China, India, Indonesia, Persia, the Danube Valley, Greece, Rome, and many other parts of the world. Hitherto, what Europe has learnt from Asia has been part of the Indian, Chinese, Japanese or Indonesian Great Traditions. It is not the task of formal education to transmit Little Traditions, as distinct from knowledge about them and awareness of their presence.

Since the nature of contemporary British society is 'multicultural' and has been so for at least two centuries, the introduction of the serious study of world musics in schools could be a distinctively British characteristic of music education in the United Kingdom: it would recognize the varied cultural origins of the country's citizens and the many life-styles that coexist, while at the same time stimulating a sense of national unity by means of the common interest in musical exploration and experience. The presence of African and Asian musics has value in the context of the European Great Tradition because they are novel and technically different systems. If, however, they are promoted for social reasons, simply because there are persons of African and Asian origin living in the country, their value is immediately debased. In effect, they would be reclassified as a Little Tradition of Europe, and the opportunity of fruitful dialogue with the Great Traditions of Africa and Asia would thereby be lost.

The development of music education in schools has created new contexts for all kinds of music-making. Neither British folk music nor Pakistani, Indian and Caribbean musics can be taught or presented in 'the appropriate cultural context'. It is neither desirable nor practical to develop in the United Kingdom systems of education appropriate for life in other parts of the world – and a strict interpretation of the concept of 'multicultural education' means that there should be parallel *systems* of enculturation. In any case, it is not the business of British schools to prepare its children for life in Pakistan or the Punjab any more than it was their business to prepare my grandmother to return to the Warsaw Ghetto. But it *is* their business to prepare them for full participation in the social, economic, political and artistic life of the United Kingdom and of the world at large.

Thus in the context of the United Kingdom in 1985, World Music Education is the appropriate equivalent of Kodály's Hungarian Music Education for the Hungary of 1945. There is no contradiction in the idea of teaching world musics to promote national unity. An emphasis on individual composers and performers, and a global view of the musical conventions that they have used and use, are the surest means of developing the musical consciousness of the nation in ways that will help to adapt and strengthen 'the British character' for life in the twenty-first century. Of course, it requires an act of faith in the power of musical symbols. Such an enterprise will never succeed if it is multi*cultural*: it must be multi*musical*. It can only be successful when people are touched by the aesthetic force of music and can transcend its social and cultural analogues.

A policy of teaching the best of the world's music, as well as that of the European tradition, both includes the heritage of members of the new British nation and looks forward and outward to parts of the world that have not been specifically involved in the British experience.

It is a policy that was articulated most clearly by Percy Grainger, and he developed it largely as a result of his confrontation with the beautiful unwritten music and highly original 'folk' musicians of the British Isles.

Grainger's 'universalist outlook' on music and his idea of music as a universal language of the future are possible because human beings have the mental equipment to feel beyond the cultural trappings of the different worlds of music to the common humanity which inspired the music. Thus music can become a universal language when individuals are acquainted with all forms of artistic musical expression, and through the transformation of individuals it becomes a 'vehicle for world peace and the unification of mankind' (Balough 1982:49).

APPENDIX A

A Commonsense View of all Music

by Percy Grainger

This synopsis of twelve illustrated lectures was printed in 1934 by the Australian Broadcasting Commission. The lectures were delivered twice weekly in Melbourne and relayed through national stations. They are reprinted here because they are relevant to the argument of this book, they provide an excellent insight into Percy Grainger's ethnomusicological thinking and into the kinds of music that interested him, and they are no less appropriate in 1986 as an introduction to world music.

LECTURE 1
THE UNIVERSALIST ATTITUDE TOWARD MUSIC

It seems to me that the commonsense view of music is to approach all the world's available music with an open mind, just as we approach the world's literature or painting or philosophy. It seems to me that we should be willing, even eager, to hear everything we can of all kinds of music, from whatever quarter and whatever era, in order that we may find out from experience whether or not it carries any spiritual message for us as individuals.

We are continually hearing that 'music is a universal language', yet the facts prove that music, as practised and enjoyed to-day, is the most parochial and least universal of the arts. The only European art-music we know really well is that written between 1700 and 1900, while we are quite needlessly ignorant of folk-music, primitive music and the great art-musics of Asia.

A few years ago it was difficult to find much information about the beginnings of European music or to get first-hand experience of Asiatic music. Nowadays, with ample gramophone records of exotic music and recently published books of musical

research, our sources of information are many and inexpensive.*
There is no longer any necessity for the appalling ignorance that
darkens our musical life and for all the prejudices that arise out
of that ignorance.

What would we think of a Professor of Literature who knew
nothing of Homer, the Icelandic sagas, the Japanese Heiki
Monogatori, Chaucer, Dante and Edgar Lee Masters? We would
think him a joke. Yet we see nothing strange in a Professor of
Music who knows nothing of primitive music and folk-music,
the music of mediaeval Europe, and the great art-musics of Asia,
and who knows next to nothing of contemporary music. We
should not expect a theatre to prosper that ignored the life of today and presented no plays (such as those by Shakespeare or
Euripides) that are older than 1700. Yet we think it quite natural
that our concert programmes seldom give us anything written
before 1700 and that hardly any representative compositions by
the greatest living composers are heard – with the exception of
a few futuristic compositions of an aesthetically scandalous
nature or works possessing touristic interest, such as 'The
London Symphony' by Vaughan Williams or the 'Soviet Iron
Foundry' piece by a contemporary Russian. The glorious beauties
of the 500 years of European art-music preceding Bach, the vital
interests of the myriad types of noble music that lie outside of
Europe, the soul-stirring message of the best twentieth century
music – all this is a dead letter to most of us. The object of these
twelve lectures is to let in a little light upon these neglected
branches of great music. Therefore I shall avoid, as far as possible,
the already well-known musical literature, so that I may devote
all my time to those equally great master-works that are as yet
unknown, or comparatively so. In presenting to you these unfamiliar branches of the world's best music, I shall endeavour not
to concentrate too much upon a single aspect of music (such as

* Such as: 'Geschichte der Musik in Beispielen' (History of Music by means
of Musical Examples), by Arnold Schering (Breitkopf and Haertel, Leipzig, 1931);
'Worcester Mediaeval Harmony' (of the thirteenth and fourteenth centuries), by
Dom Anselm Hughes, O.S.B. (The Plainsong and Mediaeval Music Society,
Nashdom Abbey, Burnham, Bucks, England, 1928); 'Musik des Orients' (Album
of twenty-four gramophone records of Oriental Music from Japan to Tunis, with
explanatory foreword by Prof. Dr. E. M. von Hornbostel) (Carl Lindstrom, A. G.
Kulturabteilung, Berlin, S.O. 36). The price of these publications ranges from 25/-
to £3 each.

Javanese music) in a single lecture, but shall spread several examples of each type of music over several lectures, so that your ears may have an opportunity of hearing each type of unfamiliar music more than once.

In this first lecture I want to give you a bird's-eye view of the many different types of music that I shall be presenting more fully to you in the lectures to follow.

First of all there are primitive music and folk-music, which are not written down in any kind of musical notation and therefore are inclined to vary more or less in each performance. Art-music, of course, is any type of music that is written down in any kind of musical notation, or performed according to some set formula, and therefore varies less, or not at all, from performance to performance. Art-music, being created solely or mainly by a single composer, develops great individuality in him, but suppresses individuality in the performer. (That is one of the reasons why our virtuoso performers so often fight shy of the noblest types of art-music – because they do not afford them the opportunity for individualistic personal display that they crave as public performers.)

Primitive music and folk-music, on the other hand, encourage almost unlimited individuality in the performer, to such an extent that it is hard to say, with such music, where the creative and executive roles begin and end. If a folk-singer has a voice with a wide tonal range, he freely extends melodies to show off the full compass of his voice. If he has a voice with a small range, he narrows the compass of his tunes.

Undoubtedly the world's most lovely melodies are found in folk-song, or in music (like the Javanese) that lies midway between folk-music and art-music. This is quite natural. Folk-songs are, in almost all cases, melodies without accompaniment of any kind, and the folk-singer, singing entirely alone, is able to concentrate all his creative powers upon expression in a single line – by which I mean the curves and contrasts of sound given out by a single voice or instrument. Composers of fully-developed art-music, on the other hand, cannot concentrate upon melodic expression, because they have so many other forms of musical expression to think about, such as harmony, musical form, the tone-colour and blends of various instruments, dramatic considerations, and the like. All these various aspects greatly enrich art-music, and make up for the poverty of its melodic invention. So it is with no hostility toward art-music (the music that I worship above all others) that I say that I can rarely show melodies that can vie with the best folk-songs in melodic vitality, beauty and inventiveness.

Music, like drawing and painting, seems to be neither helped nor hindered by what we call civilisation. Although we find music flourishing in fullest perfection amid great civilisations, such as those of China and Europe, we also find music of a thoroughly perfect and satisfying kind amongst the most primitive savages – just as we find glorious drawings by the primitive Bushmen in Africa and bafflingly lovely paintings in the stone-age caves of Alta Mira, in Spain. Thus the Australian Aborigines have tunes that are lithe and graceful as snakes, and highly complex in their rhythmic irregularities. You will hear some of these on gramophone records made by Dr. E. Harold Davies, of the University of Adelaide.

In some kinds of primitive music the voices of men call to each other as wild animals call to each other in the jungle, sometimes one echoing or imitating the other, and thus show us the beginnings of those art-music forms that we call Imitation, Canon, Round, Catch, Fugue. African echo-music, for example, has a weird loveliness all its own.

Most of us know some of the great European Cathedrals by name or by sight and when we travel in Europe we generally spend some time looking at them. If we are musical, it is likely that we ask ourselves some question like this: 'I wonder what kind of music resounded in these cathedrals when they were new; when the whole life of mediaeval Europe centred round the church, its functions and festivities?' The answer to this question is provided by a wonderful book recently published by the Plainsong and Mediaeval Music Society in England: *Worcester Mediaeval Harmony*, by Dom Anselm Hughes. This Benedictine Monk has deciphered from old vellums over 100 pieces of music that were sung in Worcester Cathedral in the thirteenth and fourteenth centuries. One is not surprised to find that this music has the same spiritual grandeur, complexity and subtlety that we admire in the architecture of the cathedrals themselves – for it would be idle to suppose that the men who could conceive the gothic masterpieces of Europe were unable to fill those great structures with suitable devotional music. This thirteenth century Worcester music is not merely of great historical interest, but is living music worthy of being placed beside the noblest religious and spiritual music of Palestrina, Bach, Wagner or Delius. A gramophone record which I have of it was made by the monks of Nashdom Abbey, Burnham, Bucks, England, conducted by Dom Anselm Hughes, the inspired musicologist who deciphered the vellums.

One of these pieces is called 'Beata viscera'. It is one of the earliest authentic examples we have of European harmony, yet, as we hear it, there is nothing crude or imperfect about it. Robert Donnington is right when he tells us that as far back as we are able to go in the decipherable music of Europe all is perfect expressibility.

Religious vocal music of similar spiritual fervour and musical richness and complexity prevailed in Europe for 500 years after the period first mentioned and, during this period, instrumental music of a most noble and spiritual nature flourished as an off-shoot from the tree of religious music. This melodiously many-voiced instrumental music reached its zenith in the deeply emotional Fantasies for string instruments by such English composers as William Byrd, John Jenkins, William Lawes and Henry Purcell.

The credit for the discovery of these matchless examples of noblest chamber-music goes to that many-sided genius, Arnold Dolmetsch, who – like a veritable music Confucius – has opened our ears to the glories of much forgotten great music.

Purcell's masterpieces in the Fantasy form are now published in the Curwen Edition, edited by Peter Warlock and André Mangeot. In my opinion there are no later compositions for string quartet that compare with these in spiritual beauty and perfect suitability to string tone until we reach the best string writing of the twentieth century. The Purcell three-part, four-part and five-part Fantasies for strings were composed five years before Bach was born.

That Bach knew and practised similar noble traditions of string writing is evident from the Air (for string quartet) from his Overture No. 3. This is the exquisite original that is degraded and distorted in the arrangement known as the 'Air for the G String'.

After Bach's time the noblest traditions of chamber music

were lost for nearly two centuries, to be regained around 1900 by Herman Sandby, the Danish composer. The whole development, decline and recovery of European string music will be dealt with in my seventh lecture.

Perhaps music is not an art that we are justified in regarding as beginning gropingly and clumsily and gradually working its way up to skill and maturity. I believe that all races are genuinely musical, at all times and places, and that each phase of human existence brings forth its own perfect musical expression. I believe that all opinions to the contrary are due merely to our shocking ignorance of the myriad sorts of music flourishing everywhere on the earth.

Many of us have Chinese and Japanese objects of art in our homes, Persian carpets, and the like. Most of us are directly or indirectly influenced mentally by Oriental religions and lines of thought, such as those we find in Theosophy and in Gandhi's Passive Resistance. Is it likely that the races that have given us religions such as Buddhism and Hinduism, literature such as the Veddas, architecture such as the Temples of Southern India and Java and the Anghor Vat, practical systems such as ju-jitsu, have nothing comparable to offer us in music? The moment we examine the various musics of Asia we discover that they are quite on a par with Asiatic achievements in other aesthetic fields. Their various forms will be treated in subsequent lectures. Javanese music is probably the most spiritually lovely music of the Orient, if not of the whole world. It was from listening to such gong-orchestra music as this in the late 'eighties that Debussy learnt the lesson of delicacy and repose through which he was able to turn the face of modern music, around the turn of the century, in the direction of beauty and refinement – away from the noisiness and vulgarity it had taken on in the hands of many Italian, Austrian and German composers of the eighteenth and nine-teenth centuries.

Kipling and other authors write of the poetic charm exerted by the temple bells of the Far-East, but many of us are still in the dark as to how they actually sound. It is worth finding out; in doing so, compare the kind of clangourous bell-music that obtains in Bali with that of other parts. Although Bali is geographically so close to Java, we see that the strident mood of its bell-music is realms removed from the nirvana-like rapture of the Javanese gong-music.

In Indian music we can trace the origins of the coloratura singing in Italian operas, these traditions of florid Asiatic singing most probably having entered Europe with the Moors in Spain.

In contrast to pure Asiatic art-music (into which no European musical influence enters) there is the world's Hybrid Music, in which native melodic habits blend with European harmonic influences. Natives in Africa, Madagascar, the South Seas, etc., had (we may safely presume) no harmony of their own, but were quick to acquire the habit of singing in parts from Europeans – oftenest from four-part hymns that Christian missionaries brought to them. Our habits of harmony became quickly twisted to native mentality and taste, often with results of ravishing beauty. As more and more native races become half-civilised we may expect more and more of this delicious hybrid music to arise. Probably it will play a very large part in the music of the future. Already it has enriched our own world of music considerably, influencing many of our finest composers.

For the sake of illustration, take the Madagascan composition 'Oay Lahy E'; it combines a sweet freshness of melody with methods of part-writing that sound highly original to a European ear.*

The most complex hybrid music known to me is that of Raratonga, in the Cook Islands. Rushing along at breakneck speed, it combines Bach-like polyphonic complexities with discords that remind us of the most modern European art-music.

Some Raratongans were brought to an Exhibition in Christchurch, New Zealand, early in this century. Part of their performance was to recite the names of their chiefs, down the centuries. Some Maoris from Otaki heard them do this, and became vastly excited when they heard the names of their own far-back chiefs appear in the list. (This is not so surprising, seeing that the Maoris are supposed to have passed through Raratonga on their way to New Zealand, some 500 years ago.) The Maoris took the clothes off their own backs and gave them to the Raratongans (who, coming from a warmer climate, were scantily clothed), whereupon the Raratongans rose to their feet and sang songs of thanks for the gifts. This was gramophoned, on the spot, by A. J. Knocks, of Otaki.

---

* Gramophone records: 'Mampahory' and 'Oay Lahy E', Chant Malgache 50–1597–8, Disque 'Gramophone' (French 'His Master's Voice').

Somewhat akin to this hybrid music are the folk-harmonis-ations of Europe and America. We do not know exactly how these systems of improvised harmonisation arose amongst musically untutored Russian peasants and American Negroes, but it seems reasonable to assume that they are off-shoots of art-music: the folk-musician carrying away by ear strains of harmony heard in church services in both countries, and developing from these beginnings his own system of harmonic improvisation, which gradually wandered fairly far away from its prototype and finally give us original beauties and distinct procedures of its own. Interesting examples are 'Kindling Wood' (from 'Great Russian Songs in Folk-harmonisation', by E. Lineva, Moscow, 1921) (three women's voices); 'Lullaby' (from Negro Folk-songs, Hampton Series, G. Schirmer, Inc., New York) (eight mixed voices).

Believing as I do that music is always perfect amongst all races, at all times and in all places, I cannot admit any conception of musical progress that sees music passing gradually from worse to better, and which therefore belittles primitive music or the earliest traceable beginnings of art-music. On the other hand, I clearly see another kind of progress running through every kind of known music, the path and goal of which progress I shall particularly endeavour to trace in these lectures. Just as human thought begins with superstition and leads through religion towards science, so does music start with highly artificial and rule-clad forms and works persistently towards ever greater freedom and irregularity.

It seems that it is the goal of all the arts to be able, eventually, to tally the freedom and irregularity of nature as man experiences it — to be able to express through art man's reaction to the multitudinous and never-twice-repeated impressions he draws from life all around him. And just as sculpture went through a stage of very restricted and artificial representations of human and animal forms (the face and legs in profile, while the torso was shown 'front face') and gradually evolved to the Greek technique that could present bodies from all angles and in all phases of arrested movement, so music, apparently, is engaged in dis-entangling itself from the limitations imposed by scale, harmony, rhythm and arbitrary forms until it is able to copy accurately all the irregular sounds heard in nature (including human life, of course) and out of these liberated sounds evolve a musical language that can voice the surging instincts of man's musical soul and mirror the flights of his spiritual fancy.

- In this kind of progress, sliding intervals, intervals closer than the half-tone, irregular rhythms and the toleration of more and more discordant combinations of sounds play a leading part. An American Jazz example of sliding intervals is Duke Ellington's 'Creole Love Call'.

In Arthur Fickenscher's 'The Seventh Quintet' we find an exquisite and inspired use of intervals closer than our usual ones. Fickenscher, a living American composer, is one of the greatest creative giants of our era.

Cyril Scott, the exquisite English composer, has done some epoch-making experiments with highly irregular rhythms, especially in his great Piano Sonata, Op. 66.

The whole question of the goal of musical progress will be gone into in my twelfth lecture.

In presenting some rare and somewhat inaccessible types of music I wish to acknowledge my great indebtedness to the erudition and helpfulness of Professor Gustave Reese, Lecturer on Mediaeval and Renaissance Music in the College of Fine Arts, New York University.

I shall be glad to state the sources of all the music used in these lectures (the titles of gramophone records and publications) to anyone writing in for this information.

Musical illustrations in first lecture: –

Purcell: Fantasy for 4 Strings, No. 8 (string quartet).
Bach: Air in D, from Overture No. 3 (string quartet).
A. Fickenscher: Excerpts from 'The Seventh Quintet' (string quartet and piano).
Lineva: 'Kindling Wood' (three women's voices).
N. Curtis-Burlin: 'Lullaby' for eight mixed voices (four women's, four men's voices).

LECTURE 2
SCALES IN THE PAST, THE PRESENT AND THE FUTURE

We can imagine the music of the future consisting of free and unpredetermined melodic lines of sound – swooping through tonal space in gradual curves as a bird sails through the air, untrammelled by those arbitrary divisions of tone called scales. In such free music all tone might be in a state of endless flux and it is easy to imagine such music as being capable of more soulful expressiveness than any past or existing music. Indeed, there are many indications that modern music is veering in the direction of such intervallic freedom. In the Hawaiian guitar, in jazz, in the elastic intonation of saxophones, in Cyril Scott's writings for strings, in many types of popular singing, we encounter scooping and sliding sounds that are preparing the way for a departure from fixed intervals. The further we go in modernity (whether popular or classical) the more indefinite all intervallic conceptions become, and the closer intervals are to one another. The further we go backward into the past, on the other hand, the more definite are all intervals, and the greater the distance between them.

The most primitive known scale seems to be that with only two divisions to the octave, consisting of the intervals one and five. One would hardly think this a promising vehicle for composition, yet some of the most beautiful melodies are clearly influenced by this scale. In one winsome Javanese melody all the chief notes of the tune consist of one and five, all the other notes being mere embellishments or passing notes.

Slightly less primitive scales add one more interval to those already mentioned, so that we get three-tone scales, consisting of one–three–five, one–four–five, and the like. The Negro-American tune upon which Delius has based his poetic orchestral piece 'Appalachia' uses only one–three–five throughout three-fourths of its length, and many Russian, British and American folk-tunes are chiefly based upon the one–four–five scale.

Then we come to the more filled-up scales, consisting of four and five tones to the octave.

The five-tone scales are found over large areas of the world, uniting, musically, countries as far apart as China, Great Britain and America. In their melodic instincts the British and the

Scandinavians are much closer to the Chinese and other Mongolian peoples than they are to Europeans, such as the French, the Italians and the Germans. Thus an art-music composer like Cyril Scott composed melodies in the five-tone scale even before he had familiarity with British folk-songs.

These British melodious habits have been transplanted to America to such an extent that when a German-Jewish composer writes an American popular tune he couches it largely in the five-tone scale (e.g., in 'Bedelia').

The five-tone scale is equally popular in Scandinavia. Quite unconsciously Grieg writes the opening phrase of his 'To the Spring-time' in the five-tone scale. Likewise the opening of the exquisite slow movement of the Danish composer Herman Sandby's Second String Quartet is strictly in the five-tone scale – unconsciously, of course.

The modes of English folk-song and the Church modes present great problems and invite study.

So far the scales considered all belong to what are called 'gapped' scales – scales with gaps, or wide jumps, between their intervals.

The more Southern and Central peoples of Europe, in contrast to us of more Northern-European origin, use mainly filled-up scales in their melodies; they use the diatonic scales, consisting of seven notes (divided into whole-tones and half-tones) to the octave, and the chromatic scale (consisting only of half-tones) with twelve notes to the octave.

The church-modes belong to the filled-up scales and their influence upon art-music is indisputable (cf. Purcell Quartet and other works).

The influence of the chromatic scale upon harmony should be noted, too. Chromatic harmony admits the 'nature-sounds' into music and prepares the way for gliding and indefinite intervals, e.g., Nordic Nature-music (examples from Grieg, Delius, Scott, Sandby).

A curious procedure is the combination of chromatic harmonies with five-tone scale melodies in Scandinavian, British, American and Negro-American music.

(Example 'Listen to de Lambs', male quartet).

For examples of early chromaticism, note Thos. Tomkins' Fantasy, six strings.

Musical illustrations, second lecture: –

Purcell (composed 1680): Four-part Fantasy No. 4 (string quartet).

Sandby (Danish, b. 1881): Andante amoroso, 2nd quartet (string quartet).

Thos. Tomkins (English, 17th cent.): Fantasy (two violins, two violas, two 'cellos).

Excerpts from Howard Brockway's 'Lonesome Tunes' and 'Twenty Kentucky Mountain Songs' (voice and piano).

LECTURE 3
THE MONGOLIAN AND MOHAMMEDAN INFLUENCES UPON EUROPEAN MUSIC

In Asia we encounter two main types of music, the Mongolian and the Mohammedan. The Mongolian music is generally calm and solemn in mood, favours long-sustained, unadorned notes, eschews arabesques and 'fireworks' of all kinds, and shows a marked trend towards harmony. These characteristics are well in evidence in Chinese music itself, and wherever Chinese musical influence has made itself felt; for instance, in Japan, Siam, Java.

The music of the Mohammedan peoples is diametrically opposed to that of the Mongolians: the Mohammedan is restless, active and aggressive in mood, delights in arabesques, display-passages and technical dexterity, prefers short, shifting, fluttering notes, and shows little if any instinct for harmony. We might sum up the two musics thus: the Mongolian music has a simple, set, straightforward surface, with an undercurrent of deep, complex musical thought below, while the Mohammedan music has a simple substratum of musical thought, with a surface of bewildering agitation and complexity of detail.

Each music has its own especial charm and expressiveness. The Mohammedan is unsurpassed in its poignancy and passion, while the Mongolian is unique in its heroic grandeur and dreamy reposefulness.

It would seem as if these two traditions of Asiatic music have converged upon Europe 'like a pair of pincers' (to use a phrase we so often read in the Great War), the Mongolian traditions (stretching across Siberia and Russia to the Nordic lands) profoundly influencing the musical habits of the Northern European peoples, while the Mohammedan traditions have demonstrably entered Southern Europe by way of the Moors in Spain and by way of the gypsies in Eastern Europe, being clearly responsible for myriad manifestations we see in Hungarian music, in Italian operatic vocalism and in all such elements in keyboard music (Couperin, Bach, Chopin) as are offshoots of lute music – the lute being a Mohammedan instrument, called 'el oudh' in Arabic.

It is worth noting that wherever the Mongolian musical influences most abound in Europe (Scandinavia, Russia, Scotland, Ireland, etc.) we frequently encounter a quasi-Mongolian type of face, with high cheekbones, small, slightly upturned noses, and calm, smooth looks. Where the Mohammedan musical influences most prevail in Europe, we find, for the most part, larger, more prominent and more hawk-like noses, smaller cheekbones and a more aggressive facial expression.

Not only are a large majority of the folk-melodies and art-melodies of the North of Europe cast in the same scales as those prevailing in the Mongolian tradition, but the beginnings of harmony in Northern Europe are almost identical with Chinese harmony – both systems being based on the use of bare fourths and fifths. This is a very important point when we remember that the leading musicologists of Europe (men such as Hugo Riemann, Knud Jeppesen, Dom Anselm Hughes) are insisting more and more that the origin of European harmony and many-voicedness must be looked for in North-Western Europe – in Scandinavia, the Celtic lands, England, Flanders, and the North of France.

Observe the stoicism of ancient Scandinavian art (the Sagas) and of the modern Scandinavian peoples. It is somewhat similar to that of Far-Easterners. It is easy to hear the spiritual likeness between a typical Chinese melody, such as 'Beautiful Fresh Flower', and the opening of the slow movement of Grieg's C minor Sonata for violin and piano. Such a quasi-Mongolian mood (so utterly different from the moods prevailing in Southern-European music) rules a large part of Grieg's and other Scandinavian music, and it is no less frequent in British and American folk-song.

'Little Sparrow' and 'The Demon Lover' are two examples of the Kentucky folk-songs collected and exquisitely arranged by the American composer, Howard Brockway. If not told in advance that they were Kentuckian we might readily believe them to be Chinese melodies.

This stoical mood, this absence of passion, this graceful winsomeness of melodic line, not only informs Nordic folk-music, but is a foremost quality of the five hundred or more years of noble Northern European art-music that foreruns Bach.

An account of the Mohammedan elements in European music could be epitomised as follows: – The likeness of the Coloratura in Spanish gypsy music to that of India; survival of Moorish elements in Spain (comparison of Egyptian and Tunisian compositions with 'Iberia' by Albeniz); Mohammedan influence seen in piano music; and the indebtedness of modern Russian music to Mohammedan musical influences, traced through a comparison of a Persian record (cf. 'Musik des Orients') with themes in Balakirev's 'Thamar' and 'Islamey' and Rimsky-Korsakoff's 'Scheherazade'.

LECTURE 4
MELODY VERSUS RHYTHM

Quotation from Chinese 'Record of Rites', said to date from 2255 B.C.: 'Poetry is the expression of earnest thought, and singing is the pro-longed utterance of that expression'.

That statement is just as true of the higher flights of Western music to-day or yesterday as it presumably was of Chinese music long ago. I take it for granted that it is the office of the higher flights of music to uplift us, to emotionalise us and to awaken and increase within us the wellsprings of dreaminess, lovingness and compassionateness – in other words, to prepare our natures for some kind of angelic life (presumably here on earth) and to turn our thoughts away from the wordly and 'practical' things of life.

It seems evident to me that it is melody and harmony rather than rhythm that are empowered to turn our natures towards the angelic state. What do we mean by melody? I think we all mean fundamentally the same thing by the term 'melody'. Even the most unmusical person will hardly speak of a 'melody on the bugle' or 'a melody on the drum'; so we may assume that even the popular conception of melody does not associate melody primarily with broken chords or with rhythms. Melody, I take it, is single-line sound that follows the nature of the human voice. The human voice occasionally gives out shouts, barking noises and other detached sounds: but in the main it favours long, continuous sustained legato sounds – 'Prolonged utterances' – and it is these sounds that we call melody.

Instruments that closely follow the sustained utterance of the human voice (such as the strings, the saxophone, the brass and wind instruments, the organ) we consider melodious instruments; while other instruments that are not modelled upon the tone-type of the human voice (such as the piano, the percussion and plucked instruments) we consider less melodious.

Rhythm is a greater energiser, a great slave-driver; and the lower types of mankind (the tyrants, the greedy ones, the business-minded people) have not been slow to sense the practical advantages to be drawn from rhythmically-regular music as an energising, action-promoting force. When these 'hard-headed' practical people want young men to go and get themselves killed, they play marches to them; and they encourage sailors and road-workers to sing at their jobs in order that the maximum of hard work may be forthcoming as economically as possible. The practical-minded people welcome any type of music that will encourage themselves and others to dance rather than to dream, to act rather than to think.

During the last thirty years there has been a regular orgy of rhythmic music, both in the jazz and in the classical fields. Well, the results are before us, and we of the dreamy and anti-active persuasions may ask if they really are so good – from even a 'practical' standpoint. Mankind has responded most loyally to rhythmic intoxication: millions have been killed or had their lives upset by the wars and still more millions have allowed themselves to become needlessly and uselessly 'hard-boiled' in all sorts of ways – responding to the calls of energy and worldliness. We may now ask ourselves whether we should have been worse off, from any standpoint, if we had listened less to the energising suggestions of rhythm and more to the spiritualising influences of melody. Would we have done worse if we had copied Walt Whitman when he said: 'I loafe and invite my soul'?

As dance music is often designed to remind the dancers of repetitions in their dance-figures by means of repetitions of musical phrases, it stands to reason that sequential and repetitious phrases (example: Second theme of the first movement of Schubert's Unfinished Symphony) may be expected in such music. On the other hand, such sequential and repetitious phrases (and the lack of intervallic inventiveness and inspiration that they imply) are the bane of all true melody. Melody makes its chief appeal by means of slowly-moving, freely-curved, non-repetitious intervallic expression – by means of the contrasts between higher and lower notes and the subtle suggestions and meanings that these contrasts possess for musical ears, if they are heard at not too fast a speed.

Examples of pure melody: –

Plain Song (Columbia History of Music for Ear and Eye, Vol. 1.).
'Fraanar Ormen' (Archaic Norwegian hero-song).
Javanese melody ('Musik des Orients', No. 9).
Claude Le Jeune (Belgian, b. 1528): 'Pretty Swallow' (irregular rhythms).
Opening theme of Wagner's 'Parsifal' Prelude.
Melody from Cyril Scott's 'Aubade' (orchestra).

Poly-melodic music is that in which several melodies are heard at the same time, without regard for the ensuing harmonic results. Such procedure is effective with a scale like the Javanese five-tone scale, because each note of this scale harmonises with all the other notes of the scale.

Such poly-melodic music may be thought of as somewhat akin to a life lived in a kindly country where bananas grow (without human tending) naturally on the trees and life may be lived happily and selfishly without much awareness of relatives, laws, duties and the needs and troubles of our fellow-men. We see that animals can witness the death and misfortunes of their fellow-animals and go their way wholly, or comparatively, unaffected. Yet if we modern humans witness an automobile or other accident we are likely to feel deadly sick – an accident to a fellow-man being only different in degree from an accident to ourselves, so much are we aware of the world's agony all around us and correspondingly sensitized by that awareness. A similar sensitized awareness underlies Western Melodious Polyphony. As we play our own sounds in chamber music we are aware of all the other sounds around us and aware of the harmonic import of the whole. We move in a kind of blissful agony of rapturous, compassionate sound-awareness that I believe to be highly contributory to the coming angelicness of mankind.

Examples of western melodious polyphony: –

Wm. Lawes (English, d. 1645): concluding passage of Fantasy and Air No. 1 (six strings).

Bach, D sharp minor Fugue, Second Book, Well-tempered Clavier (piano).

J. Jenkins (English, 1592–1676): Fantasy 1 (five strings).

Bach, Air from Suite 3 (four strings).

It seems strange that the most perfect example of modern Melodious Polyphony that I can find should be the work of a modern German; for we might expect that the 'Sachlichkeit' (practical-mindedness) of present-day Germany would hardly make for angelic music. Yet the fact remains that the first movement of Hindemith's 'Die Junge Magd' carries on in great perfection the noblest old-time polyphonic traditions and unites with them a harmonic freedom (a harmonic discordance) that is a clear twentieth century gain.

In such melodiously polyphonic music all the voices that make up the harmonic texture are equally expressive melodically: the bass (lowest) part is as melodious as the top part and the middle parts are not less so.

(Example: Hindemith's 'Die Junge Magd', opening passage for string quartet.)

The slave-driving, soul-stultifying influence of rhythm lies in regularity and repetitiousness and in all the four-bar phrases and other forms of musical platitudinousness and inventive torpor that these give rise to. On the other hand, subtle, irregular, unrepetitious rhythms hold fine influences toward freedom and rapture.

Examples of melodious irregular rhythm: –

Cyril Scott: 'Solemn Dance' for six strings, piano, harmonium, bells.

Cl. Le Jeune (Belgian, b. 1528): 'Pretty Swallow', six voices.

LECTURE 5
SUBLIME AND FRIVOLOUS ELEMENTS IN MUSIC

Broadly speaking, I think we may generalise and say that religious music, all over the world (whether in Europe, Asia, the South Seas, or elsewhere), has been preponderatingly melodic – as we should naturally expect lofty and uplifting music to be. On the other hand, the dance songs and the working songs of the world have been comparatively rhythmic and unmelodic.

For hundreds of years in Europe noble traditions of religious and spiritual music prevailed. Composers knew when they were dealing with lofty subjects that their music would have to consist mainly of long notes and sustained sonorities and that rhythmic appeals would have to take a very secondary place.

But, during and after Bach's time, such strong influences from dance music and popular music beat down upon art-music that most of the noblest traditions of art-music were forgotten or ignored. It was a real jazz-period – much as if we, to-day, were to throw overboard the accumulated musical culture found in Palestrina, Bach, Wagner, Delius, etc., and content ourselves merely with such cultural traditions as survive in Gershwin and other gifted half-jazz-like composers. (Such jazz traditions would be no mean ones; yet they would inevitably prove much more limited than traditions derived from the totality of all available musical traditions of all kinds.)

It was only after Mendelssohn, Schumann and others in the mid-nineteenth century had discovered and appraised the grander flights of Bach's genius (and that of his forerunners) that a competent insight into the nobler technical and emotional possibilities of true art-music was regained.

Bach himself (in spite of the vulgarising influences that beat down upon him) knew quite well when to use the nobler or the less noble musical traditions. When he dealt with a devotional chorale, such as 'Ich ruf' zu Dir', he used long, sustained sonorities and avoided rhythmic effects; but when he wrote dance music he used the short tones and rhythmic possibilities of such a type to the full.

Great composers in culturally well-balanced periods divide their creative activities between various types of musical expression. But in certain periods the instinct for balance becomes upset, and we then find undue pre-occupation with just one side of music. Thus, Domenico Scarlatti seemed well-nigh indifferent to all except florid display-music, while Frederick Delius, on the other hand, stoops to nothing below soulful music of the very loftiest kind.

One of the peculiarities of jazz, as we have experienced it during the last fifteen or more years, has been the attempt to force all types of musical thought to conform to the narrow confines of current dance forms – the most undancelike types of 'classical', or other, music being adapted (jazzed) to that end. Somewhat before, and during the Hadyn–Mozart–Beethoven period, a rather similar dancification overtook almost all forms of art-music, and that is why I take the liberty of calling these three great composers 'The jazz classics'. The habits and traditions that had governed religious and other emotional music for a thousand years or more in Europe were set aside overnight in favour of the vulgar traditions of dance music, and other popular 'active' music.

Haydn, Mozart, and Beethoven, knowing (or conforming to) few traditions other than those of active music, were seldom able to sustain a solemn, dreamy or spiritual mood for more than a few brief moments. They were, therefore, seldom able to write a typical slow movement, judged by the standards of earlier and later geniuses. In the thirty-two Beethoven piano Sonatas I can discover only one genuine slow movement (displaying the sustained emotion, singing sonority and reposeful continuity of type as we find them in the slow movements of de Machaut, Byrd, Bach, Brahms, Delius, and in the art-music of Java and India) – the first movement of the so-called 'Moonlight Sonata'.

(Examine the slow movements of the Beethoven piano Sonatas.)

It is hard for us more serious-minded twentieth century composers to understand the childishness with which vulgar tune-types were introduced into the most serious art-music a little over a hundred years ago. Admirers of Beethoven, who consider the Ninth Symphony one of his loftiest achievements, will hardly deny that the tune associated with the words beginning 'Freude, schoener Goetterfunken, Tochter aus Elysium' (Joy, lovely divine spark, daughter from Elysium) plays a highly important role in the climax of the whole symphony. Yet this tune is so close to that of 'Yankee Doodle' in line, rhythm, type and form, that the one forms a perfect continuation to the other. Yet all attempts to make 'Yankee Doodle' an official American national anthem have been vetoed on the ground that it is too frivolous, vulgar and undignified for such use, while the conventional opinion regarding the Beethoven theme is that it is suitable thematic material for incorporation in one of music's sublimest creations!

The frivolousness of Haydn's approach to the symphony is well instanced by the unexpected whack on the drum in the 'Surprise Symphony' (imagine the soul-benefit derived by the innocent listener from such a nerve-shock!) and by that last movement in which one orchestral player after another blows out his candle and leaves the orchestra, until 'the end is silence'. Beethoven's 'The Wrath over the lost Farthing' is an example of a similar 'low-brow' attitude; as if it were the office of music (the most angelic of the arts) to remind mankind of its miserable money!

The attitude I am taking towards the 'jazz-classics' is not in any sense original or personal with me. I am merely voicing the usual opinion of composers of my generation. I do not know a single distinguished modern composer who places Beethoven high among the great composer-geniuses; though no thoughtful musician would deny his superlative gifts. Debussy's aesthetic repudiation of Beethoven is too well known to need quoting.

That Beethoven, in his last works, was continually reaching out for more soulful forms of expression than the musical idioms of his day provided is evident enough. But it stands to reason that his deeply inspired individual yearnings for more sublime musical utterance were constantly frustrated by his unfamiliarity with musical traditions dealing with long, sustained, singing notes and phrases. The shortcomings of Beethoven's late works are too often laid at the door of his growing deafness. Surely it would be more sensible to attribute them to his lack of musical culture, to his ignorance of the great musical resources of the past.

A mountain that starts to rise out of a low plain is not likely to equal the heights reached by a mountain that starts to rise in the midst of an elevated mountain chain. The worship of individualism in the nineteenth century favoured the idea of a single individual, unaided by great cultural backing, rising single-handedly to the greatest heights. An age of 'self-made men' in the economic field liked the idea of self-made men in music also. But I believe that any ample study of musical history will reveal the fact that music at its best is always a cumulative, rather than an individualistic, affair. Knud Jeppesen wrote of Palestrina: 'In him all the streams run together', and this is true of all those other greatest composers who satisfy most and longest. An art like music cannot prosper fully when its roots are cut away from under it.

When the composers that followed after Bach wilfully cut themselves loose from all the rich traditions of sublime music that had accumulated in an unbroken continuity for at least 900 years (possibly much longer), in order to concentrate solely, or mainly, on the pretty-prettiness and lively appeal of active music (when − to put it slightly otherwise − they abandoned a singing, sustained type of sonority in favour of short, jerky, hammering sounds), they were committing some kind of artistic suicide. And it was only when the grandeurs of Bach's sublimest muse were revealed by Mendelssohn's performance of the 'Matthew Passion', in the early middle of the past century, that composers such as Chopin, Schumann, Wagner, César Franck, and Brahms began to repossess the full heritage of all the musical ages, and thus were able to express mankind's loftiest emotions in a musical language adequate to such a task.

In rating the finest traditions of art-music above those of dance music I am not in the least deaf to the charms of the latter. We may enjoy the appeal of a straw-thatched farm-house as sincerely as we admire the architectural grandeurs of a cathedral − but we enjoy it in a different way. The purpose of this lecture is to distinguish, musically speaking, between farm-houses and cathedrals. The 'farm-house' type of appeal can be studied in the following examples of Nordic dance music: −

Grieg: Norwegian Dances (piano duet).
Piano pieces by Grainger and David Guion.
Roger Quilter: Three English Dances (piano duet).
John Powell: 'Natchez-on-the-Hill' (two pianos).

LECTURE 6
THE SUPERIORITY OF NORDIC MUSIC

My approach to music has always been a cosmopolitan one. As a boy I loved Bach above all other composers. In my early 'teens I worshipped Wagner and Brahms. I did not come in contact with Nordic art-music and folk-music until all my musical tastes were formed – formed upon the German classics. Yet the more I study what I can get hold of of the world's music, the more convinced I am that the white races have as yet produced no music that can vie with Nordic music, at least in depth, intensity, beauty and complexity.

Many well-wishers of British music, however generously they may feel or act towards that music, still think of British music as trailing behind the best Continental music in quality and quantity. I am sure that this typically British view of British music is far too modest. Trained as I have been on Continental standards, and inquisitive as I have always been towards every phase of the music of the whole world, I can only see that Nordic (British, Scandinavian, American) folk-songs out-sing all other folk-songs in their sheer melodic beauty and that Nordic art-music composers, from the thirteenth century to the present day, out-soar all others in the purity, grandeur, complexity and compassionate emotionality of their musical speech.

It is interesting to consider what is Nordic, and to what extent certain German, Russian, Jewish and French composers should be classed as Nordics; and to note the almost invariable blue-eyedness of the greatest British, American, German and Russian composers.

The loftiness and complexity of Northern music should be observed, together with the gradual fading of loftiness into frivolousness and simplicity as we move southward in European music. Thus the greater loftiness of German (especially North-German) composers should be compared with the frivolousness of Austrian composers.

Why it has been difficult to get a hearing for Nordic music: the non-Nordic musicians have been in the saddle as executants, conductors, etc., for the last 200 years and they are unable to understand the depth and complexity of our Nordic music;

for, as Goethe said, 'No man can understand greatness greater than his own.'

The lonely pursuits of Nordic life (shepherding and the like; the isolated farm-house which is the typical rural mode of dwelling in Scandinavia, Ireland, Great Britain, America, Australia, etc. – whereas most French, German and Italian peasants live closely packed together in villages) have had a far-reaching effect upon our folk-songs; for a singer, singing alone by himself, can use the full range of his voice, whereas tribal or village tunes (sung in unison by several singers) are limited upwards by the low-pitched voices and limited downwards by the high-pitched voices. Such tribal tunes often have a compass of a mere half-octave, while the Nordic folk-songs of the lonely pursuits often enjoy a range of close upon two octaves.

The close-to-nature life of the Nordic peoples is equally evident in their art-music. Nature-sounds (such as the wailing of the wind) have found their way into Nordic art-music as into no other – especially since nineteenth century chromaticism made possible in music a close approximation to such nature-sounds.

(For examples of wailing sounds, and other nature-sounds, see Grieg, Delius, Sandby, etc.)

Musical illustrations of Nordic music: –

Ole Bull: Saeterjentens Sondag (violin or 'cello and harmonium).

My Lagan Love (Irish folksong, arr. by Hamilton Harty), mezzo-soprano and piano.

Vermlandsvisan (Swedish air, 'cello and piano).

Delius: Dance Rhapsody, two pianos.

Wm. Lawes (English, died 1645): Fantasy and Air, No. 1 (six strings).

Sandby (Danish, b. 1881): Slow movement, second string quartet.

Cyril Scott: Piano Sonata (lecturer).

English, 13th century; 'Puellare Gremium', six voices (from 'Worcester Mediaeval Harmony', by Dom Anselm Hughes).

Delius: 'The Wind Soughs in the Trees' (from 'North Country Sketches', piano duet).

Appendix A

THE DEVELOPMENT OF EUROPEAN STRING MUSIC

The path of the development of European string music may be clearly traced from the thirteenth century to the present day. My main contentions concerning European music (the apparent affinity of Mongolian and Nordic musical traditions, the reputed Northern origin of harmony and polyphony, the emotional and technical superiority of Nordic music) having been dealt with in previous lectures, this lecture will consist almost entirely of musical examples, with short descriptions of each number and its place in musical history.

In this lecture the prodigious life-work of Arnold Dolmetsch will be appraised. This great master-musician (musicologist, lecturer, instrument-maker and inspired interpreter) – drawing his entire remarkable family into the task – has done more than any other living man to make many periods of older European music 'live' again.

Examples of development of string music: –

Two early 'Conducti' (13th century), three strings.
Josquin des Prez (Netherlands, born about 1450): 'La Bernardina' (three strings).
Jean Japart (Netherlands): 'Nenciozza mia' (about 1500), four strings.
William Byrd (English, born 1543): Fantasy for six viols.
Gramophone records of 'chest of viols', played by the Dolmetsch family (Columbia).
J. Jenkins (English, born 1592): Fantasy for five viols.
Purcell (English, born 1658): Four-part Fantasy, No. 2.
Sandby (Danish, born 1881): 'Serenade', for six strings; 'The Elfhill', seven strings and harmonium.
Gabriel Fauré (French, 1845–1924): Extract from Second Quartet (piano and strings).

The chests of viols (used by the pre-Bach English chamber music composers) were perfectly balanced, the whole family of viols being used in its completeness. The original quartet of the violin family (as written for by Henry Purcell, and consisting of treble, alto, tenor and bass violins) also was complete and properly balanced. But the modern quartet (lacking, as it does, the tenor violin – which should fill in the gap between the viola and the 'cello) is top-heavy and unbalanced. What would we think of a choir that contained no tenor voices? The unbalanced make-up of the conventional string quartet is one of the reasons why the quartets of Haydn, Mozart, Beethoven, Brahms, etc., do not compare in tonal beauty with string compositions of the older English chamber music composers who wrote for perfectly balanced combinations of stringed instruments.

LECTURE 8
ECHO-MUSIC

Imitations of echo-sounds (as heard in nature), and the echoing of one voice by another, naturally played a great part in primitive music, and these habits have found their way into art-music and given us some of the finest art-forms we know. This process may be traced clearly in the following examples: –

> Zulu Love Song (two men's voices), from Natalie Curtis-Burlin's 'Songs and Tales from the Dark Continent' (G. Schirmer, New York).
>
> G. de Machaut (French, born 1300): Ballade No. 17 (three men's voices).
>
> Josquin des Prez (Netherlands, born about 1450): Canon, 'A l'heure' (string quartet).
>
> Adrian Willaert (Netherlands, born about 1480): 'O salutaris hostia' (alto voice, tenor voice, string quartet).
>
> William Brade (English, born 1560): Allemande (six strings).
>
> Bach: A minor Fugue (Well-tempered Clavier, Book 1) (four pianists at two pianos).
>
> Stravinsky: Excerpt from 'Petrouchka' (two pianos).
>
> Grainger: Excerpts from 'Lord Peter's Stable-boy', and 'The Warriors' (two pianos).

LECTURE 9
VARIOUS SYSTEMS OF HARMONY

This lecture will endeavour to demonstrate the different systems of harmony, as they exist in various times and places, and to combat the theory that European harmony began crudely and worked its way gradually up to perfection; I shall try also to show that each system of harmony has its own special advantages and perfections and that there is a gain and a corresponding loss with each change in harmonic habits. Examples: –

Early English: 'Fowles in the Frith' (about 1240), (tenor voice, bass voice).

Similarity of Chinese harmony and early European organum.

Five-tone scale harmony (Yasser), (harmonium).

13th century English Fauxbourdon: 'Beata viscera' (gramophone), (recorded by Dom Anselm Hughes and the Monks of Nashdom Abbey, Bucks., England).

13th century English melodious polyphony: 'Alleluya psallat' (gramophone, Dom. A. Hughes' recording).

Polymelodic Harmony in Java (gramophone).

Early European discords (de Machaut, etc.).

16th century concords: Le Jeune's 'Pretty Swallow' six voices).

Late 19th century concords: Cyril Scott's 'An Old Song Ended' (voice and piano), and 'The Garden of Soul-Sympathy' (from 'Poems' for piano).

16th century, contrasted concords and discords: Palestrina's 'Mori quasi il mio core' (four mixed voices).

Drone-harmony in Africa, Scotland, Norway (piano, lecturer).

Russian folk-harmonisation: Lineva's 'The Flowers that Bloomed in the Field' (four mixed voices).

Russian Church-harmonisation: Rachmaninoff's 'Laud Ye the Name of the Lord' (eight mixed voices).

Negro folk-harmonisation: Curtis-Burlin's 'Lullaby' (eight voices), and 'Listen to de Lambs' (four men's voices).

Hybrid harmony from Raratonga and Madagascar (gramophone).

'Unnatural' harmonisation (in which the harmonies, whether concordant or discordant, run counter to

the harmonic suggestions of the melody).
(Examples: Grieg, Delius, Grainger, on piano).
'Atonal' Harmony: Schönberg (piano).

LECTURE 10
SONGS WITH INSTRUMENTAL ACCOMPANIMENT

The folk-songs of Northern Europe are well-nigh always without instrumental accompaniment; so it seems reasonable to suppose that European song with instrumental accompaniment is an off-shoot of the Mohammedan musical traditions that entered Europe with the Moors – for Mohammedan music abounds in the co-operation of a few instruments with a single voice. It will be seen that records of Mohammedan music show much the same sort of instrumental preludings and interludes that we find in European accompanied song. Example of Spanish lute accompaniment: 'Paseábase el rey moro' (Diego Pisador, c. 1550). In the southern parts of Western Europe the lute (introduced into Europe by the Moors) was for centuries the most popular instrument for accompanying the voice, and the lute technique has left a deep imprint upon the piano accompaniments to our songs. Instance: Fauré's 'Après un rêve'. But the more Northerly European countries – always, it would seem, more intrinsically melodious (and polyphonically melodious) than the Southern – were much given to accompanying a voice with melodious instruments, such as the strings. The gradual development of songs with instrumental accompaniment is unfolded with the following illustrations:

German (1460): 'Aus fahr ich hin' (baritone voice and viola).

Lyonel Power (English, 1420): 'Anima mea', for mezzo-soprano and three strings.

G. Dufay (Netherlands, 1400–1474): 'Softly the Day and the Season Fall Asleep' (baritone or mezzo-soprano voice and three strings).

Heinrich Finck (German, 1445–1527): 'O schönes Weib', tenor voice and three strings.

F. Corteccia (Italian, died 1538): 'O Glorious, Golden Era', tenor voice, two violas, two 'cellos.

Paul Hindemith (German, b. 1895): 'Die Junge Magd'

(first section), for mezzo-soprano and string quartet
(flute, clarinet, ad lib.).
Roger Quilter (English, b. 1877): 'Weep ye no more,
Sad Fountains' (example of perfect modern song,
voice and piano).

Natural and 'denatured' singing constitute another interesting
aspect of song, and will be discussed in this lecture.

LECTURE 11
'TUNEFUL PERCUSSION'

The term 'tuneful percussion' is used to describe all percussion
instruments with clear intonation and therefore capable of playing tunes (in contradiction to those percussion instruments, such
as drums and cymbals, that have indefinite or unclear pitch, and
therefore cannot play tunes).

The tuneful percussion instruments of Asia, Africa and South
America include the Indian cup-bells, Bali bell-orchestras,
Javanese gong-orchestras, Oriental xylophones, South American
marimbas, and many others. Of late years the bell-makers of
Europe and America have adapted many Asiatic and other exotic
tuneful-percussion instruments to our European pitch and scale
requirements, with the result that we are able to decipher
Oriental music from gramophone records and perform them on
these Europeanized Oriental instruments whenever we want to.
I have tried the experiment of orchestrating Debussy's 'Pagodas'
(the piano piece he wrote after studying the Javanese gong-
orchestras at a Paris exhibition around 1888) for a complete
tuneful percussion group – thus, as it were, turning back to its
Oriental beginnings the Asiatic music he transcribed for a
Western instrument (the piano). In so doing I am merely giving
it back to the sound-type from which it originally emerged.

Musical illustration: –

Debussy's 'Pagodas' on piano.
Debussy's 'Pagodas' on tuneful percussion group (one
harmonium, one celesta, one dulcitone, six pianists
on three pianos, one xylophone, three players on
metal marimba, three players on wooden marimba,
one staff-bells, one glockenspiel).

Ravel's 'The Valley of Bells' and 'Le Gibet' (piano).
Grainger: 'Eastern Intermezzo' for percussion group
(20 players).

LECTURE 12
THE GOAL OF MUSICAL PROGRESS

This lecture will be a full unfolding of my ideas about musical progress (that music must progress technically until it is able to tally the irregularities and complexity of nature) touched upon in Lecture 1. The following processes will be traced down the ages: The filling up of gapped scales, the closer and closer approximation of intervals, the ever-increasing discordance of what we consider 'harmony', the irregularisation of rhythm, the breaking up of artificial musical forms (Fugue form, Sonata forms, etc.), the increasing use of sliding intervals – all moving in the direction of 'free music'.

The progress from artificial, formal, rule-clad music to 'free music' corresponds to man's progress from fear-inspired spirit-worship (and other superstitions) to a fear-free scientific conception of life. Superstitious man fears storms at sea (they say that there are no poems exulting in storms at sea more than a hundred odd years old), and so is unlikely to write 'sea-music'. Modern scientific-mooded man is romantically drawn to storms at sea (as to all other manifestations of the nature-forces) and therefore writes 'sea-music' and welcomes the sounds of storms into his music.

As long as primitive, superstitious man feared nature he prized human company and shunned solitude. Modern scientific man (growing to love nature as he studies her) welcomes solitude in nature and glories in the vastness and non-humanness of the universe. All this shows in modern music – in the titles of Nordic art-music (Delius's 'The Song of the High Hills', Sandby's 'Sea-Mood', etc.) and in the manner in which the Nordic composers take up the scale-less, sliding, discordant nature-sounds into their music.

'Free music' (towards which all musical progress clearly points) will be the full musical expression of the scientific nature-worship begun by the Greeks and carried forward by the Nordic races. It will be the musical counterpart of Nordic pioneering, athleticism, nudism.

In all these respects it will be cosmic and impersonal, and thus fundamentally differentiated from the strongly personal and 'dramatic' music of non-Nordic Europe with its emphasis upon sex, possession, ambition, jealousy and strife.

Illustrations of various phases of musical progress: –

Gliding tones in Grieg, Sandby, Cyril Scott, and Jazz (string quartet and piano).

Irregular rhythms: Cyril Scott's piano Sonata, Grainger's 'Hillsong 2' (two pianos).

Discordant harmony: Schönberg and others.

Intervals closer than half-tones: Fickenscher's 'The Seventh Quintet' (piano and string quartet).

Grainger: Example of 'Free Music'.

Musical Transcription

by Percy Grainger

The transcription below is given as an example of Percy Grainger's meticulous attention to detail. It is taken from his paper on 'Collecting with the Phonograph', *Journal of the Folk song Society*, III/iii, no. 12, May 1908.

BOLD WILLIAM TAYLOR.

SUNG BY MR. GEORGE GOULDTHORPE,

Phonographed and noted by Percy Grainger. AT BRIGG, LINCOLNSHIRE, JULY 28TH, 1906.

Sung in G. M.M. ♩ = between 108 & 120. *The time very even, and with lilt.*

(1) I'll sing you a song a - bout two lŏv - ers, O, from Lich-fied-eld (field)

town thă (they) căme; O the young... man's năme was Will-yum Tăy-lor, The

mă - a - den's năme was Sa - rah Grăy. (2) Now for...... a sol - dier

Will-yum's list - ed, For... a sol - dier he 'as gône, he's

gône and left sweet lŏv - e - lĭ (lovely) Săl - ly For te (to) sigh a-den (and)

fŏer (for) to mourn. (3) Săl - ly's pa - rents thă - e (they) con-trolled 'er,

Filled 'er heart full of grief and woe, And then at last she

vow - ed an' said For a sol - dier she would go. (4) She

dressed her-self in man's ap - pa - ril, Man's ap - pa - ri - del

She put on, And for to seek bold Will - yum Tay - lor, And

for te (to) seek hi—m she 'as gône. (5) Wôn (one) dãy... as she wâs

ex - er - cis - in', Ex - er - cis - in' a - mongst the rest, With a

sil - ver chẽ - an (chain) hung down her wã - ast - coat And

there he spied her... milk white breast. (6) And

then... the cap - tain he stepped up to her, Asked her what had

brought her there. "I've côme te seek my own trẽ - ö (true) lôv - er,

He has proved to...... me so vẽre." (severe) (7) "If you've

côme... tè seek yer own true lŏv - er, Prăy tell to

me his nāme." "His nāme it is bold Will - yum Tay - lor,

O from Lĕ - ich - fie - deld town he cāme." (8) "If his

nāme it is bold Will-yum Tay - lor, And he has proved tŏ

you so vēre; He's got mar - ri - ed to an Ir - ish lā - dy,

He got mar - ri - ed the o - ther yēcr. (year) (9) If you rise ear - li

in the morn - in', Ear - ly by the break of dāy, There

you shall spy bold Will - yum Tāy - lor Walk - in' with this

lā - dy gāy." (10) Then she rose ear - li in the morn - in',

Ear - ly by the brēk (break) of dāy; And there she spied bold

Will - yum Tay - lor, Walk - in' with this lā - dy gāy. (11) And

then she called for a brāce of pis - tils, Λ

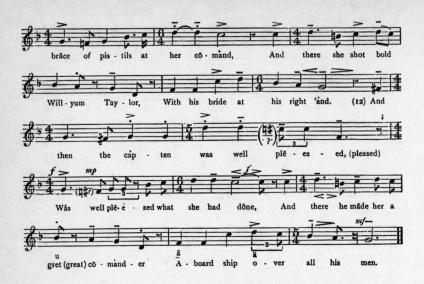

bráce of pis - tils at   her cō - mànd,   And   there she shot bold

Will - yum   Tay - lor,   With his bride   at   his right 'ànd.   (12) And

then   the   cáp - ten   was   well   plē - ez - ed, (pleased)

Wâs   well plē- e - zed what she had   dône,   And there he màde her a

gret (great) cō - mànd - er   A - board ship o - ver   all his   men.

Notes

1. A tape-recording of examples of different genres of Venda music is available from the University of Washington Press, Seattle, Washington 98195, USA. Further references to this tape in the text will be described as 'Venda tape'.
2. Venda tape, side 2, 17b
3. See Appendix B.
4. Frederick Fennell and Eastman Wind Ensemble: *Hill-Song number 2*. Included on US: Mercury Golden Imports SR1 75011
5. *Come Day, Go Day, God Send Sunday*. Songs by John Maguire. Leader LEE 4062 (1973). Notes by Robin Morton
6. *Music of Africa* series no. 8, Uganda, LF 1173, side 2, nos. 2 and 3
7. *Babylon by Bus*. Bob Marley and the Wailers. Tuff Gong Records, 56, Hope Road, Kingston, Jamaica
8. Venda tape, side 1, 2e. See also *Venda Children's Songs* (Blacking 1967), nos. 4, 30, 31 and 56
9. Venda tape, side 2, 13
10. Venda tape, side 1, 9e
11. Venda tape, side 2, 18d. See also Blacking 1969 and 1970.
12. Venda tape, side 1, 1, 5, 6; side 2, 22
13. *Music of Africa* series no. 8, Uganda, LF 1173, side 2, nos. 5 and 7
14. *Musique Malinké*, recorded by Gilbert Rouget, Collection Musée de l'Homme. Disques Vogue, LDM 30113
15. Many recordings of Chopi music are available in *The Sound of Africa* series.
16. *Inuit Games and Songs*. Unesco collection *Musical Sources*. Philips 6586 036
17. *Me dawo ase*. Compositions by Papa Oyeah MacKenzie. 1981, Love Power Records, Areacem (Paris), PP2
18. *Amadu Bansang Jobarteh, Master of the Kora*. 1978, Eavadisc EDM 101. Cambridge Audio-Visual Ethnomusicological Archive
19. Fine examples of African composer-performers can be found on: *Music of Africa* series no. 6, The African Music Society's Choice for 1952, especially side 1, nos. 1, 2 and 4; side 2, no. 2 (see also scores in John Blacking, 1955, 'Eight Flute Tunes from Butembo',

African Music 2(4), pp. 26–43); *The Soul of Mbira* and *Shona Mbira Music*, Nonesuch records H–72054 and H–72077, recorded in the field by Paul Berliner, and *Mbira Music of Rhodesia*, performed by Dumisani Maraire, University of Washington Press, Seattle; recordings of the Nkomi harpist Rampano Mathurin in Pierre Sallée, 1978, *Deux études sur la musique du Gabon*, Paris: O.R.S.T.O.M., document no. 85.

Bibliography

Abercrombie, David (1965). *Studies in Phonetics and Linguistics*. London: Oxford University Press.

Allen, Warren Dwight (1962). *Philosophies of Music History: a Study of General Histories of Music, 1600–1960*. New York: Dover Publications. 2nd edn. [c. 1939]

Anderson, Lois Ann (1968). 'The MIKO Modal System of Kiganda Xylophone Music'. 2 volumes. Unpublished PhD thesis, University of California, Los Angeles.

Balough, Teresa (1982). *A Musical Genius from Australia*. Selected Writings by and about Percy Grainger. Music Monographs, no. 4. Nedlands: University of Western Australia Press.

(1982A). 'Grainger as Author – a Philosophical Expression', *Studies in Music*, no. 16. Percy Grainger Centennial Volume. Nedlands: University of Western Australia Press.

Barkóczi, Ilona and Csaba Pléh (1982). *Music Makes a Difference*. Budapest: Zoltán Kodály Pedagogical Institute of Music.

Bateson, Gregory (1973). *Steps to an Ecology of Mind*. St Albans: Paladin.

Baxandall, Michael (1972). *Painting and Experience in Fifteenth Century Italy*. Oxford: Clarendon Press.

Beaudry, Nicole (1978). 'Toward Transcription and Analysis of Inuit Throat-games: Micro-structure', *Ethnomusicology*, 22(2), pp. 261–73.

(1980). 'Arctic Throat-games: a Contest of Song', *Performing Arts in Canada*, 17(3), pp. 26–8.

Becking, Gustav (1928). *Der musikalische Rhythmus als Erkenntnisquelle*. Augsburg: B. Filser.

Bernstein, Leonard (1976). *The Unanswered Question*. Cambridge: Harvard University Press.

Bird, John (1982). *Percy Grainger*. Victoria: Sun Books. [c. 1976]

Blacking, John (1962). 'Musical Expeditions of the Venda', *African Music*, 3(1), pp. 54–78.

(1967). *Venda Children's Songs: a Study in Ethnomusicological Analysis*. Johannesburg: Witwatersrand University Press.

187

(1969A). *Process and Product in Human Society*. Johannesburg: Witwatersrand University Press.

(1969B). 'Songs, Dances, Mimes and Symbolism of Venda Girls' Initiation Schools', Parts 1–4, *African Studies*, 28.

(1970). 'Tonal Organization in the Music of Two Venda Initiation Schools', *Ethnomusicology*, 14(1), pp. 1–54.

(1971). 'Music and the Historical Process in Vendaland'. In K. P. Wachsmann (ed.), *Music and history in Africa*. Evanston: Northwestern University Press, pp. 185–212.

(1973). *How Musical is Man?* Seattle: University of Washington Press. 2nd edn 1976, Faber and Faber.

(1976). 'Dance, Conceptual Thought and Production in the Archaeological Record'. In G. de G. Sieveking, I. H. Longworth and K. E. Wilson (eds.), *Problems in Economic and Social Archaeology*. London: Duckworth, pp. 3–13.

(1980). 'Trends in the Black Music of South Africa, 1959–1969'. In Elizabeth May (ed.), *Musics of Many Cultures*. Berkeley: University of California Press, pp. 195–231.

(1981). 'Political and Musical Freedom in the Music of some Black South African Churches'. In L. Holy and M. Stuchlik (eds.), *The Structure of Folk Models*, ASA Monograph no. 20. London: Academic Press, pp. 35–62.

(1981A). 'The Problem of "Ethnic" Perceptions in the Semiotics of Music'. In Wendy Steiner (ed.), *The Sign in Music and Literature*. Austin: University of Texas Press, pp. 184–94.

(1983). 'The Concept of Identity and Folk Concepts of Self'. In Anita Jacobson-Widding (ed.), *Identity: Personal and Socio-Cultural*. Uppsala: Almqvist and Wiksell, pp. 47–65.

(1985). 'The Context of Venda Possession Music: Reflections on the Effectiveness of Symbols', *1985 Yearbook for Traditional Music*, pp. 64–87.

Bloch, Maurice (1974). 'Symbols, Song, Dance and Features of Articulation: Is Religion an Extreme Form of Traditional Authority?' *Archives Européennes Sociologiques*, 15, pp. 55–81.

Bose, Fritz (1966). Review of Alan P. Merriam, *The Anthropology of Music*, *Current Anthropology*, 7 (April), p. 219.

Bridges, K. M. B. (1932). 'Emotional Development in Early Infancy', *Child Development*, 3, pp. 324–41.

Bücher, Karl (1901). *Industrial Evolution*, tr. S. Morley Wickett. London: George Bell.

(1909). *Arbeit und Rhythmus*. 4th edn. Leipzig: B. G. Teubner.

Chacón Americo Valencia (1981). 'Los chiriguanos de Huancane', Boletin de Lima, separata del nos. 12–13–14.

Chase, Gilbert (1976). 'Musicology, History and Anthropology: Current Thoughts'. In John W. Grubbs (ed.), *Current Thought in Musicology*. Austin: University of Texas Press.

Clynes, Manfred (1974). 'The Pure Pulse of Musical Genius', *Psychology Today*, 1 (London, July), pp. 51–5.

(1977). *Sentics: the Touch of Emotions*. London: Souvenir Press.

Crickmore, Leon (1968). 'An Approach to the Measurement of Music Appreciation', *Journal of Research in Music Education*, 16 (3 and 4), pp. 239–53, 291–301.

Dahlhaus, Carl (1983). *Foundations of Music History*. Cambridge University Press. Tr. J. B. Robinson [c. 1967].

De Bono, Edward (1969). *The Mechanism of Mind*. London: Jonathan Cape.

Donner, Philip (1981). 'Research for the Advancement of Music in Tanzania'. In Liisa Paakkanen (ed.), *Participation, Needs, and Village-level Development*, Jipemoyo 4, Helsinki: Publication no. 18 of the Finnish National Commission for UNESCO and Institute of Development Studies, University of Helsinki.

Durkheim, Emile (1912). *Les formes élémentaires de la vie reliqieuse: le système totémique en Australie*. Paris: Alcan. Tr. J. W. Swain, New York: Collier Books, 1961.

Ehrlich, Cyril (1985). *The Music Profession in Britain since the Eighteenth Century: a Social History*. Oxford: Clarendon Press.

Ellis, A. J. (1885). 'On the Musical Scales of Various Nations', *Journal of the Society of Arts*, 33, pp. 485–527.

England, Nicholas (1967). 'Bushman Counterpoint', *International Folk Music Journal*, 19, pp. 58–66.

Euba, Akin (1974). 'Dúndún Music of the Yoruba'. PhD thesis, The University of Legon, Ghana.

Feld, Steven (1982). *Sound and Sentiment: Birds, Weeping, Poetics, and Song in Kaluli Expression*. Philadelphia: University of Pennsylvania Press.

Ferguson, Donald (1960). *Music as Metaphor*. Minneapolis: University of Minnesota Press.

Fischer, Ernst (1963). *The Necessity of Art*. Harmondsworth: Penguin.

Fromm, Erich (1961). *Marx's Concept of Man*. New York: Ungar.

Geertz, Clifford (1964). 'The Transition to Humanity'. In Sol Tax (ed.), *Horizons of Anthropology*. London: Allen and Unwin, pp. 37–48.

(1975). *The Interpretation of Cultures*. London: Hutchinson [c. 1973].

(1976). 'Art as a Cultural System', *Modern Language Notes*, 91, pp. 1473–99.

Grainger, Percy (1908). 'Collecting with the Phonograph', *Journal of the Folk Song Society*, III/iii, no. 12 (May), pp. 147–62.

(1915). 'The Impress of Personality in Unwritten Music', *The Musical Quarterly*, 1 (July), pp. 416–35.

Grebe-Vicuna, Maria-Ester (1980). 'Generative Models, Symbolic Structures, and Acculturation in the Panpipe Music of the Aymara of Tarapaca, Chile'. Unpublished PhD thesis, The Queen's University of Belfast.

Hawkes, Terence (1977). *Structuralism and Semiotics*. London: Methuen.

Herndon, Marcia and Norma McLeod (1980). *Music as Culture*. Darby Pa.: Norwood.

Hess, H. (1973). 'Is There a Theory of Art in Marx?' *Marxism Today*, 17(10), pp. 306–14.

Hillman, James (1970). 'C.G. Jung's Contributions to "Feelings and Emotions": Synopsis and Implications'. In Magda Arnold (ed.), *Feelings and Emotions*, New York: Academic Press, pp. 125–34.

Hood, Mantle (1982). *The Ethnomusicologist*. Kent State University Press.

Jones, Le Roi (1973). *Blues People*. New York: Morrow.

Katz, Ruth (1970). 'Mannerism and Cultural Change: an Ethnomusicological Example', *Current Anthropology*, 11(4–5), pp. 465–76.

Keali'inohomoku, Joann (1979). 'Culture Change: Functional and Dysfunctional Expressions of Dance, a Form of Affective Culture'. In John Blacking and Joann Keali'inohomoku (eds.), *The Performing Arts: Music and Dance*. The Hague: Mouton, pp. 47–64.

Kettle, Arnold (1972). 'The Progressive Tradition in Bourgeois Culture'. In Lee Baxandall (ed.), *Radical Perspectives in the Arts*. Harmondsworth: Penguin Books, pp. 159–74.

Kodály, Zoltán (1974). *The Selected Writings of Zoltán Kodály*. London: Boosey and Hawkes.

Labour Party (1975). *The Arts: a Discussion Document for the Labour Movement*. London: Labour Party.

Laing, Dave (1978). *The Marxist Theory of Art*. Sussex: The Harvester Press.

Lambert, Constant (1966). *Music Ho!* 3rd edn. London: Faber.

Langer, Susanne (1948). *Philosophy in a New Key*. New York: Mentor Books.

  (1953). *Feeling and Form*. London: Routledge and Kegan Paul.

Lévi-Strauss, Claude (1963). *Structural Anthropology*. New York: Basic Books.

  (1969). *The Raw and the Cooked*, tr. John and Doreen Weightman. New York: Harper Torchbook.

Linton, Patricia (1984). 'The Effects of Dance Experience on Children's Imagination and General Development in Primary Schools in Liverpool'. Unpublished PhD thesis, The Queen's University of Belfast.

Livingstone, Frank (1973). 'Did the Australopithecines Sing?' *Current Anthropology*, 14(1–2), pp. 25–9.

Lloyd, A. L. (1967). *Folksong in England*. London: Lawrence and Wishart.

Lloyd, Stephen (1982). 'Grainger's Original Compositions', *Studies in Music*, no. 16. Percy Grainger Centennial Volume. Nedlands: University of Western Australia Press, pp. 11–17.

(1982A). 'Grainger and the Frankfurt Group', *Studies in Music*, no. 16. Percy Grainger Centennial Volume. Nedlands: University of Western Australia Press, pp. 111–18.

Lomax, Alan (1968). *Folk Song Style and Culture*. Washington, D.C.: American Association for the Advancement of Science.

Lomax, Alan and Norman Berkowitz (1972). 'The Evolutionary Taxonomy of Culture', *Science* 171 (21 July), pp. 228–39.

Lukes, Steven (1973). *Emile Durkheim: his Life and Work*. London: Allen Lane.

Maslow, Abraham (1954). *Motivation and Personality*. New York: Harper.

(1964). *Religions, Values, and Peak Experiences*. Kappa Delta Pi.

Mazo, Joseph (1974). *Dance Is a Contact Sport*. New York: Da Capo.

McLean, Mervyn (1978). 'Innovations in *Waiata* Style', *1977 Yearbook of the International Folk Music Council*, vol. 9, pp. 27–37.

Mellers, Wilfrid (1950). *Music and Society*. 2nd edn. London: Dennis Dobson.

Merriam, Alan P. (1964). *The Anthropology of Music*. Evanston: Northwestern University Press.

Messner, Florian (1980). *Die Schwebungsdiaphonie in Bistrica*. Tutzing: Hans Schneider.

(1981). 'The Two-part Vocal Style on Baluan Island. Manus Province, Papua New Guinea', *Ethnomusicology*, 25(3), pp. 433–46.

Meyer, Leonard B. (1956). *Emotion and Meaning in Music*. Chicago: Chicago University Press.

Moore, Jerrold Northrop (1984). *Edward Elgar: a Creative Life*. Oxford: Oxford University Press.

Morton, Robin (1973). *Come Day, Go Day, God Send Sunday*. London: Routledge and Kegan Paul.

Mugglestone, Erica (1982). 'Guido Adler's "The Scope, Method, and Aim of Musicology" (1885): an English Translation with an Historico-analytical Commentary'. *1981 Yearbook for Traditional Music*, vol. 13, pp. 1–21.

Nattiez, Jean-Jacques (1983). 'Inuit Vocal Games', *Ethnomusicology*, 27(3), pp. 457–75.

Nettl, Bruno (1984). *The Study of Ethnomusicology: Twenty-nine Issues and Concepts*. Urbana: University of Illinois Press.

Ornstein, Robert (1973). 'Right and left thinking', *Psychology Today*, May, pp. 87–92.

Parry, C. Hubert (1896). *The Evolution of the Art of Music*. London: Kegan Paul, Trench, Trubner and Co.

Petrović, Ankica (1977). 'Ganga: a Form of Traditional Rural Singing in Yugoslavia'. Unpublished PhD thesis, The Queen's University of Belfast.

Porter, James (1976). 'Jeannie Robertson's *My Son David*, a Conceptual Performance Model', *Journal of American Folklore*, 89, pp. 7–26.

Reck, David (1977). *Music of the Whole Earth*. New York: Charles Scribner's Sons.

Redcliffe-Maud, Lord (1976). *Support for the Arts*. London: Calouste Gulbenkian Foundation.

Reeves, Helen (1982). 'A Universalist Outlook: Percy Grainger and the Cultures of Non-Western Societies', *Studies in Music*, no. 16. Percy Grainger Centennial Volume. Nedlands: University of Western Australia Press, pp. 32–52.

Rokeach, Milton (1960). *The Open and Closed Mind*. New York: Basic Books.

Rouget, Gilbert (1969). 'Sur les xylophones équiheptatoniques des Malinké'. *Revue de Musicologie*, 55(1), pp. 47–77.

    (1977). 'Music and Possession Trance'. In John Blacking (ed.), *The Anthropology of the Body*. Monograph no. 15. London: Academic Press, pp. 233–9.

    (1980). *La musique et la transe: esquisse d'une théorie générale des relations de la musique et de la possession*. Paris: Gallimard.

Sachs, Curt (1961). *The Wellsprings of Music*. The Hague: M. Nijhoff.

Schoenberg, Arnold (1951). *Style and Idea*. London: Williams and Norgate. Enlarged edn 1975.

Seeger, Charles (1957). 'Toward a Universal Sound-writing for Musicology', *Journal of the International Folk Music Council*, 9, pp. 63–6.

    (1958). 'Prescriptive and Descriptive Music Writing'. *The Musical Quarterly*, 44 (April), pp. 184–95.

Segato de Carvalho, Rita Laura (1984). 'A Folk Theory of Personality Types: Gods and Their Symbolic Representation by Members of the Sango Cult in Recife, Brazil'. Unpublished PhD thesis, The Queen's University of Belfast.

Silbermann, Alphons (1963). *The Sociology of Music*, tr. Corbet Stewart. London: Routledge and Kegan Paul.

Strongman, K.T. (1978). *The Psychology of Emotion*. 2nd edn. Chichester: John Wiley and Sons.

Tax, Meredith (1972). 'Culture Is Not Neutral, Whom Does It Serve?' In Lee Baxandall (ed.), *Radical Perspectives in the Arts*. Harmondsworth: Penguin, pp. 15–29.

Tracey, Hugh (1948). *Chopi Musicians: Their Music, Poetry, and Instruments*. London: Oxford University Press.

Trevarthen, Colwyn (1979). 'Communication and Cooperation in Early Infancy: a Description of Primary Intersubjectivity'. In Margaret Bullowa (ed.), *Before Speech*. Cambridge: Cambridge University Press, pp. 321–48.

Uzoigwe, Joshua (1981). 'The Compositional Techniques of UKOM Music of South-Eastern Nigeria'. Unpublished PhD thesis, The Queen's University of Belfast.

Van Gennep, Arnold (1960). *The Rites of Passage*, tr. Monika P. Vizadom and Gabrielle L. Caffee. London: Routledge and Kegan Paul.

Wachsmann, Klaus P. (1950). 'An Equal-stepped Tuning in a Ganda Harp', *Nature*, 165, p. 40.

Washburn, Sherwood (1968). 'Behaviour and the Origin of Man', *Proceedings of the Royal Anthropological Institute* for 1967, pp. 21–7.

Wertheimer, Max (1945). *Productive Thinking*. New York: Harper.

Westall, Robert (1975). *The Machine-Gunners*. London: Macmillan.
(1985). *Children of the Blitz: Memories of Wartime Childhood*. Harmondsworth: Viking.

Westrup, Sir Jack (1973). *An Introduction to Musical History*. 2nd edn. London: Hutchinson. [c. 1955]

Witkin, Robert (1976). *The Intelligence of Feeling*. London: Heinemann.

Young, J. Z. (1971). *An Introduction to the Study of Man*. Oxford: Clarendon Press.

Zemp, Hugo (1979). 'Aspects of 'Are'are Musical Theory', *Ethnomusicology*, 23, pp. 6–48.
(1981). 'Melanesian Solo Polyphonic Panpipe Music', *Ethnomusicology*, 25(3), pp. 383–418.

Notes on recordings

Several good introductions to ethnomusicology are easily available (e.g. Merriam 1964, Reck 1977, Herndon and McLeod 1980, and Hood 1982), and Bruno Nettl (1984) has produced a thoughtful personal statement on important issues in the discipline.

Some useful surveys of recorded examples of world music have been published and are available as follows:

(i). *The Demonstration Collection of E. M. von Hornbostel and the Berlin Phonogramm-Archiv*. Two 12-inch 33⅓ rpm discs, 1963. Produced by Indiana University Archives of Traditional Music. Ethnic Folkways Library FE 4175. Commentary by Kurt Reinhard and George List.

(ii). *Music of the World's Peoples*. Five 12-inch 33⅓ rpm discs, 1951–55. Ethnic Folkways Library FE 4504/4508. Introduction and notes by Henry Cowell.

(iii). *World Collection of Recorded Folk Music Established by Constantin Brailoiu* (1951–58). Six 12-inch 33⅓ rpm discs, 1984. International Archives of Folk Music of the Geneva Ethnographic Museum, VDE 30–425/430. Commentary by Laurent Aubert and Jean-Jacques Nattiez.

(iv). *The UNESCO Collection 'Musical Sources'* edited for the International Music Council by the International Institute for Comparative Music Studies and Documentation. General Editor: Alain Daniélou.

(v). *The Sound of Africa* series published by the International Library of African Music, I.S.E.R., Rhodes University, Grahamstown 6140, South Africa. This collection was inaugurated by Hugh Tracey in the late 1940s.

(vi). *Museum Collection Berlin (West)*. Editor: Artur Simon. Commentaries in English and German. From the Musikethnologische Abteilung, Museum für Völkerkunde. Staatliche Museen Preussischer Kulturbesitz, Stauffenbergstrasse 41, 1000 Berlin 30.

Index

195